If you want to learn Early African History
START HERE

If you want to learn Early African History
STARTHERE

AND

50 Questions & Answers about The History of Black People

BY

Robin Walker

REKLAW EDUCATION LTD
London (U.K.)

CONTENTS

PART THREE: THE AUTHOR

OPENING REMARKS

Many people have told me of their interest in early Black or African history and heritage. These people were from all walks of life--students, teachers, plumbers, nurses, civil servants, journalists, electricians, the unemployed, entrepreneurs, etcetera. Many were also parents who wanted to pass on information to their children.

What they had in common was that they were unsure of where to begin their reading and study but they still wanted to find out more information. This book was written to simplify that journey.

As the author of *When We Ruled* (UK, Reklaw Education Limited, 2013) an 818 page book on African history, I could also see the need to produce a smaller book that condenses and simplifies the information. I want to make the data as accessible as possible--hence this book.

This book is in two parts. The first part is called *If you want to learn Early African History START HERE.* The second part is called *50 Questions & Answers about The History of Black People.*

The first part of the book, *If you want to learn Early African History START HERE,* is a general introduction to Classical African history covering some of the most important ancient and medieval empires. It began life as two separate lectures that I gave to introduce African history. One of the lectures was called *When We Ruled: Thousands of Years of a Visible African Heritage.* The second lecture was called *The Lost Civilisations of Central Africa.* To write this section of the book, I combined these two lectures into one narrative. In the final part of this section, I suggest other sources that a student could read to advance their knowledge even more.

The second part of the book, *50 Questions & Answers about The History of Black People,* began life when a colleague approached me to give him an extended interview on Black or African history. The colleague posed 50 varied questions to me to which I gave extended answers. He asked me about Nile Valley history, Ancient Kingdoms and Empires, The Slave Trade, earlier Black historians and their writings, etcetera. I hope that the

50 questions answer most of the questions that people raise concerning Black or African history.

The final part of this book contains information about me and the lectures that I teach on these topics.

Read and enjoy!

Robin Walker 2014

PART ONE

IF YOU WANT TO LEARN EARLY AFRICAN HISTORY

START HERE

INTRODUCTION

A few years ago, while browsing through a book by a scholarly German, Dr Henry Barth, I was particularly struck by a scene he drew showing jungles, swamps, and wild animals (Figure 1).

If one didn't know better, this scene could stereotype Africa as a land without worthwhile history. The book was based on Dr Barth's fact-finding visit to Africa that was made in the early 1850s. He published his findings in a five-volume set called *Travels and Discoveries in North and Central Africa*. The volumes were published between 1857 and 1858.

When Africa is dismissed as a land without history, people in the Black Community often claim: Of course, we have a history! We were once slaves! Many people are aware of the role that England played in the mass enslaving of Africans from the time of Queen Elizabeth I. England's leading slave trader, Sir John Hawkins, led an important slave raid in 1562.

Figure 1. Image from Henry Barth's *Travels and Discoveries in North and Central Africa.*

This, however, raises another question: What history do Black People have before 1562?

I propose to answer this question.

IF YOU WANT TO LEARN EARLY AFRICAN HISTORY

START HERE

The Songhai Empire

The Songhai Empire, at its height, ruled two thirds of West Africa (Figure 2). Its first kings ruled in 690 AD, but the great period was from 1464 to 1591. Its important cities were Gao (the political capital), Timbuktu (the cultural capital), Djenné and Kano. At its height, the empire ruled portions of Senegal, Gambia, Guinea, Mali, Mauritania, Niger and Nigeria. There were two waterways running through the Empire, the Senegal River and the Niger River.

The Songhai Empire had writing. The Black Community has been led to believe that Africa had no writing and relied entirely on oral traditions. Tombstones from the Songhai period have survived. Some of these tombstones date back to the eleventh century AD.

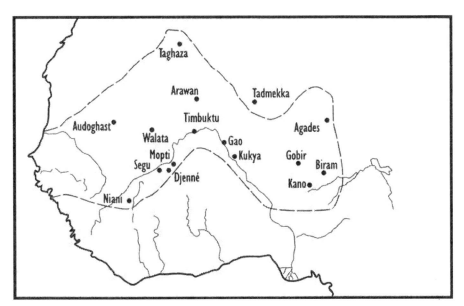

Figure 2. The Songhai Empire at its height in the sixteenth century AD.

Figure 3. City of Timbuktu from Henry Barth's *Travels and Discoveries in North and Central Africa*. Clearly, Dr Barth drew more than just swamps and wild animals!

The city of Timbuktu was a typical West African city from the period (Figure 3). It was the cultural capital of the Songhai Empire. Channel 4 Television made a documentary that claimed it had a fourteenth century population of 115,000 people. They further claimed it had a university population of 25,000 people. My research says it also had a school population of 30,000 people. These figures are not large but when it is understood that fourteenth century London had a total population of 20,000 people this shows that Timbuktu was five and a half times bigger than medieval London.

Timbuktu, like all great cities, survived because of trade. There were camel caravans, especially in the north, bringing salt into Timbuktu. There were donkey caravans, especially in the south, bringing gold into Timbuktu. Ibn Khaldun, a great medieval historian, said that on just one trade road there were 12,000 camels operating in a single year. Goods also moved by water. There were barges that carried from three to 50 people. There were also royal boats that carried up to 80 people. Some watercrafts had cabins where whole families cooked, ate and slept.

Gold was the most important trading product in the Songhai Empire. Salt was the second most important. It was mined in the northern city of Taghaza and carried south by camel caravan. In many parts of West Africa, luxury saltcellars were made and are still held by many European museums. Leather was another important trading product. Kano was the centre of this industry. In this city, they made leather pillowcases,

Home   >   REVEALED: the richest person ever!

REVEALED: the richest person ever!

THE African king whose £250bn empire, says a new inflation-adjusted survey, was worth three times Bill Gates's fortune.

By: Julie Carpenter and Simon Edge
Published: Wed, October 17, 2012   Comments   Like {0}   Tweet {0}   +1 {0}

The King of Kings: Mansa Musa I had the golden touch in West Africa

1. MANSA MUSA I - £249bn (1280-1337) Musa, whose title Mansa meant "king of kings", ruled the Mali Empire (a large part of West Africa and including the city of Timbuktu) which provided half the world's supply of gold from three huge mines. A devout Muslim, he established Mali as an intellectual hub of the world.

2. ROTHSCHILD FAMILY - £217bn (1744 onwards) The European banking dynasty was begun by Mayer Amschel Rothschild, who was born in a Jewish ghetto in Frankfurt. The son of a merchant, he set up a finance house and installed each of his five sons in the five main European financial centres. In the UK, Nathan Meyer Rothschild almost single-handedly financed the British war effort against Napoleon and reputedly won a greater fortune speculating that Wellington would win at Waterloo.

Figure 4. Some new information on Mansa Musa I from the *Daily Express*.

bookcases, saddles, boots and slippers. Some of these leather products were collected by the British Museum in the mid-nineteenth century. Among the British Museum artefacts are ostrich feather sandals as well as boots and leggings. Leo Africanus, a contemporary of the Songhai Empire, commented on Hausaland's shoe industry as early as 1526.

As large as the gold industry, the salt industry, and the leather industries were, the biggest industry in medieval West Africa was ... books! This is what Leo Africanus, a Moroccan contemporary, had to say on the book trade of Timbuktu in 1526: "In Timbuktu there are numerous judges, PhDs, and clerics, all receiving good salaries from the king. He pays great respect to men of learning. There is a big demand for books imported from North Africa. More profit is made from the book trade than any other line of business."

Black families and institutions still have many of these old books as family heirlooms. There are 3,450 old manuscripts still surviving in the cities of Chinguetti and Ouadane. There are perhaps 6,000 manuscripts in the city of Walata. There are an astonishing 700,000 surviving manuscripts in Timbuktu. It is thought that a quarter of these books are about law. Others were about the Koran, history, logic, ethics, biographies, mathematics, astronomy and astrology, medicine and geography.

With these multiple sources of wealth: the gold trade, the salt trade, the leather trade and the book trade, rulers would proudly display their wealth. There was a famous map drawn in 1375 called the Catalan Atlas. The West African ruler is depicted on the map with a golden crown, an orb of gold, and a wand of gold. The king, Mansa Musa I, was rumoured to be the richest man on the face of the earth (Figure 4).

As powerful rulers did elsewhere, the West African kings built great monuments. The Great Mosque of Djenné (Figure 5) began life as a palace in the eleventh century AD. It was converted into a mosque in 1204. The building was largely destroyed in the 1820s and was fully restored in 1907. It was made of sun-baked bricks that formed the inner shell of the walls. Wooden buttresses were built into the walls to add strength and this was covered over by hand with plaster. This is a style of architecture called Western Sudanic. This is roughly contemporaneous with the European style of Gothic. Half of the building is columned inside but the rest is courtyard. At 56 square metres, it is the largest clay brick building on earth.

A few of the palaces have survived from that period as palaces. One good example still standing is the royal palace in the city of Daura. It has maintained its original plan, but has been added to. Each new ruler commissioned additional buildings to the original construction. The palace complex is essentially an estate of buildings.

The houses in Djenné are typical examples of villas that have survived from the Songhai period. The houses were usually of two stories with 5 to 6 rooms. They date back to at least the fifteenth century. One of the upstairs

Figure 5. Model of the Great Mosque of Djenné in the Bamako Museum, Mali.

rooms was a *salanga* or toilet. It is worth remembering that in sixteenth century London if you walked past someone's open window you had better duck!

You would have no idea what might be coming out of that window!

Great Benin

Other civilisations flourished near the West African coast. Great Benin was located in southern Nigeria and flourished from 900 to 1897 AD. Benin City was its capital (Figure 6).

At its height in the fifteenth and sixteenth centuries, Benin City was an impressive metropolis. It was 20 to 24 miles in circumference and had 30 broad and straight streets. It was laid out approximately on a horizontal vertical grid. On one side of the city was the Palace of the Oba or King, almost a whole city by itself. Captain Richard Burton said that it could comfortably accommodate 15,000 people.

The scale of Benin construction was so large that it is in the *Guinness Book of Records.* The *Guinness Book of Records,* 1974, says the following: "The largest earthworks in the world carried out prior to the mechanical era were the linear boundaries of the Benin Empire." Back then, it was thought that the walling totalled 5,000 to 8,000 miles. That figure was sufficient to

Figure 6. The Nigeria region in the sixteenth century AD.

get it into the *Guinness Book of Records*. The true figure, however, is that Benin City contains a total of 10,000 miles worth of walling!

Decorating the royal palace were splendid brass plaques, the so-called 'Benin bronzes.' During the reign of Oba Oguola in the late thirteenth century, Yoruba metal art was introduced into Benin. Benin absorbed this influence and went on to produce the finest metal art of the Middle Ages. A European scholar, Professor Felix Von Lushan, described Benin Art as the very highest technical achievement possible. Another interesting feature of Benin art is that it anticipates the arts and crafts ideology of later times. They made products that were both beautiful and useful. One famous piece of work in the British Museum is a brass water container designed to look like a leopard.

Benin art depicts many different things (Figures 7, 8, 9 and 10). Some pieces depict sentries guarding the Palace of the Oba. Others show soldiers wearing body armour. Some pieces show Saharan traders on horseback. One interesting piece shows trading with Europeans with manilas as the

Figure 7. Commemoration bust of Queen Mother Idia. 16th century. (Photo: Bin im Garten).

Figure 8. Benin Bronze. 48 cm x 38 cm. (Photo: Michel Wal).

currency. The most famous piece, however, is the Queen Mother bust. Oba Esigie commissioned it in the early sixteenth century. It was probably based on his mother, Idia. Incidentally, the Queen Mother was politically powerful. A Dutch chronicler wrote: "The king undertakes nothing of importance without having sought her council."

Figure 9. Benin Bronzes. (Photo: Warofdreams).

Figure 10. Pendant Mask: 16th century. Ivory, iron, copper (?); H. 9 3/8 in. Metropolitan Museum of Art. (Photo: steve4710).

The history of Benin is divided into two dynasties. The Ogiso Dynasty ruled from about 900 until 1170 AD. This was a line of 15 rulers. The Second Dynasty ruled from 1170 until 1897 when Benin was colonised by the Europeans. During the reign of Oba Ewuare, 1440 to 1473, Benin became an empire. Ewuare's armies campaigned against 201 towns and villages in the southern Nigeria region. He captured their leaders and compelled the masses to pay tribute.

In the early days, Benin traded with the Saharan states to the north. Benin exported ivory, pepper and textiles. They imported copper and Saharan horses. After 1485, trade links were established with Portugal and the rest of Europe. Benin exported dyed cotton cloth, jasper, leopard skins, pepper, ivory, and soap. The Portuguese eventually banned West African soap to protect their own industries. The ivory products included elaborately designed saltcellars and tableware. Luxury condiments were made in Benin and other parts of West Africa at this time. European courts purchased this tableware at a handsome price.

The Kanem-Borno Empire

The Kanem-Borno Empire stretched across the Central Sahara region (Figure 11). At its height, it ruled portions of Cameroon, Nigeria, Niger, Chad, and Libya. Njimi was its first capital and Ngazargamu was its second capital.

The rulers of Kanem-Borno were called Mais and were divided into two dynasties. The Dugawa Dynasty was the first ruling dynasty. They were in power from 800 to 1075 AD. The Seifuwa Dynasty was the second ruling dynasty. They were in power from 1075 until the late 1800s when the Empire was colonised by the Europeans.

Mai Idris Alooma (1564-1596) was the most important ruler. He conquered north, south, east, and west to build the empire. He reformed and standardised the judicial system using Sharia law. He encouraged scholars from all over Africa to come to Kanem-Borno. Ruins of his Summer Palace survive today. It was commissioned by Queen Mother Amsa and built three miles away from Ngazargamu, the second capital. It was located there to separate Mai Idris Alooma from the corrupting influence of the court.

Kanem-Borno opened diplomatic relations with other civilisations. Queen Mother Amsa opened relations with Turkey. She persuaded the Turks to give Kanem-Borno firearms. The letter from the Turkish sultan to Mai Idris still exists and makes interesting reading, especially the attempt to butter up the Mai: "To the honourable emir, the most just, the most

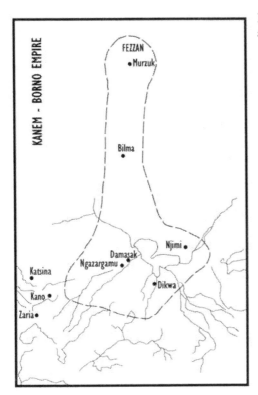

Figure 11. The Kanem-Borno Empire at its height.

exalted, the most perfect, the most noble, the most illustrious, the most magnificent, the rightly-guided, the one aided by God, the helper of the warriors among the believers, the supporter of the brave men among the adherents of the unity of God, the person enwrapped with the love of the Community, the possessor of sovereignty and sanctity, the king of the province of Borno at present, king Idris - may God prolong his prosperity and make his aims successful."

Two Englishmen visited the Empire and wrote learnedly about it. Major Dixon Denham and Captain Hugh Clapperton wrote *Narrative of Travels and Discoveries in Northern and Central Africa* published in 1826. They published sketches of the castles in the Empire. They also made sketches of Borno knights wearing chainmail and quilted armour. Cavalry was an important part of the power of the Mais. What is interesting here is that such forms of armour were used in Songhai and many other African civilisations, all the way across Africa, from west to east.

The English visitors also sketched a scene showing the royal court in session. The ruler is shown behind a cage against a castle wall. Although not visible, this cage probably had curtains, perhaps to increase the mystery

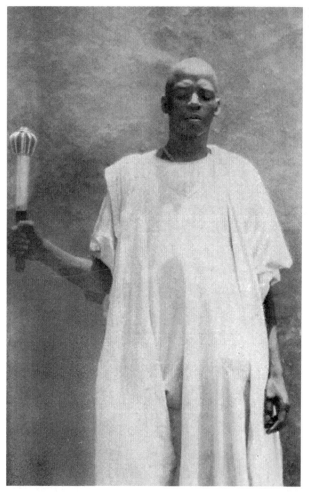

Figure 12. Royal Sceptre of the Mais.

of the ruler. On the ground in front of him are his ministers with elaborate robes, turbans and voting flags. To the side of the scene are two trumpeters in very fine robes. We know from other documents that the Empire had principal governors for the North, the South, the East, and the West, each with their own courts. We also know that the Queen Mother and the Queen's Sister, both with their own courts, held the highest positions of all. By tradition, they had even more power than the Mai.

The German scholar mentioned at the beginning, Dr Henry Barth, drew cityscapes of some of the Kanem-Borno cities. He published his findings in a five-volume work in 1857 and 1858. The city of Murzuk is shown with multi-storey buildings, truncated pyramids, and what looks like a saloon bar from the Wild West!

William Winwood Reade, another Englishman, travelled to Kanem-Borno. He followed in the footsteps of Denham and Clapperton who got there 40 years before he did. He wrote an interesting picture of what the earlier Englishman saw. It reads as follows: "Denham and Clapperton ... were astonished to find among the Negroes magnificent courts; regiments of cavalry, the horses caparisoned in silk for gala days and clad in coats of mail for war; long trains of camels laden with salt and natron and corn and cloth ... They attended with wonder the gigantic fairs in which the cotton goods of Manchester, the red cloth of Saxony, double-barrelled guns, razors, tea and sugar, Nuremberg ware and writing paper were exhibited for sale. They also found merchants who offered to cash their bills (i.e. cheques) upon houses at Tripoli; and scholars acquainted with ... the Greek philosophers."

The Munhumutapa Empire

An Englishman, John Speed, drew the first map of Africa ever published in England (Figure 13). It gave a good picture of what information was known about Africa in 1627.

Depicted on the map is a very large empire that dominated southern Africa. In Europe, this empire was called 'Monomotapa.' The map shows that Munhumutapa dominated the region that we would now call Zimbabwe, Mozambique and extended into South Africa. The Empire controlled the region from the twelfth or thirteenth centuries AD until 1629.

In France, a portrait called "Le Grand Roy Mono-Motapa" was published. The Great King is shown with a crown, a patterned cape fastened by a brooch, two bracelets, an earring and a staff. Published underneath the portrait is information about the Empire. Apparently, it was very rich in gold. We are also told that several kings were tributary to the Great King. The Empire was very large and had a circuit of 2400 miles. Interestingly idolaters, sorcerers, and thieves were very severely punished.

The cultural capital of the Empire was Great Zimbabwe. This complex consisted of 12 buildings spread over three-square miles. Most of the construction took place in the valley region. However, one of the buildings was a hilltop castle that overlooked the entire area. Although now perished, thatched cottages existed all over the three square mile region, inside and outside the walls. It is thought that 18,000 people lived there in the fourteenth century (some say 25,000). This would make the city slightly smaller (or larger) than medieval London (population 20,000).

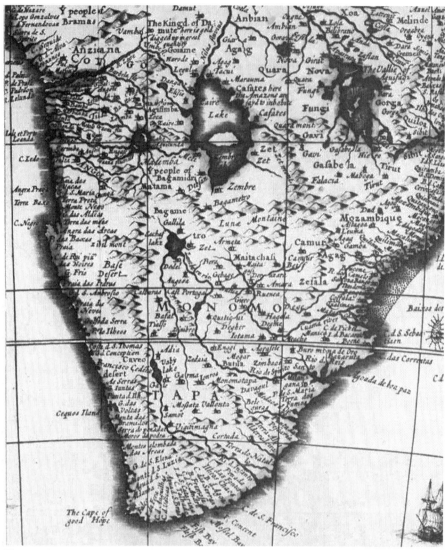

Figure 13. Portion of the John Speed map of 1627.

The central construction in the valley region is called the Temple also called the Elliptical Building (Figure 14). It has walls that are 30 feet high and 17 feet thick in places. The bricks are fashioned to hold together without the use of mortar. J. Theodore Bent, an early surveyor of the site, wrote "as a specimen of the dry builder's art it is without a parallel." The hilltop castle has walls that were more massive. These were 22 feet thick in places!

Figure 14. Inside the Great Zimbabwe Temple. (Photo: Marius Loots).

Great Zimbabwe is one of 600 ruins dotted over the regions of Zimbabwe, Mozambique and South Africa. Archaeologists have surveyed stone ruins as far south as Johannesburg. They have surveyed ruins as far east as the Mozambique Coast. They have surveyed ruins as far north as Zambia. The scope of the ruins may tell us the size of the Munhumutapa Empire. The walls of the various ruins show particular styles of construction. Some of the walling shows a chevron pattern. Other walls show a check pattern. Other walls show a dentelle pattern. The unity of styles indicates a unity of culture across the southern Africa region.

At the site of Mapungubwe, archaeologists found golden artefacts. The most impressive of these was a small golden model of a hippopotamus and a golden sceptre. Gold was mined in southern Africa since the eighth century AD. The southern Africans mined an astonishing 43 1/4 million tons of ore in medieval times. This produced 700 tons of pure gold. This is industrial scale mining produced in early times. This would have produced pure gold to the value of $7.5 billion at 1998 gold prices.

Archaeologists have also found X-shaped ingots of copper. These ingots were the currency. The people of Munhumutapa traded with the Swahili of the East African coast. They sold gold and ivory to the Swahili who, in turn, sold it to Asian countries as far as the Far East. Munhumutapa imported luxury products from the Swahili. These products originally came from Asian countries and the Far East, including Chinese porcelain. Trade fairs and bazaars were conducted along the Zambezi River.

The Swahili Confederation

On the East African coast a great culture flourished called the Swahili Confederation (Figure 15). This civilisation flourished from approximately 700 to 1505 AD. The civilisation was an important part of the Indian Ocean trade.

The great Swahili cities included Mogadishu on the coast of Somalia, Gedi on the coast of Kenya, the island of Zanzibar and finally Kilwa, both off the coast of Tanzania.

Visitors to the East African coast have been impressed by the high standard of domestic architecture. A typical East African front door had a central piece, brass bosses, and wooden floral designs. There were front doors in some of the Asian civilisations that share the same features. This raises the question: Who copied from whom?

The reason why this question is important is that there were Arab ships involved in the Indian Ocean trade. East African ships were also involved

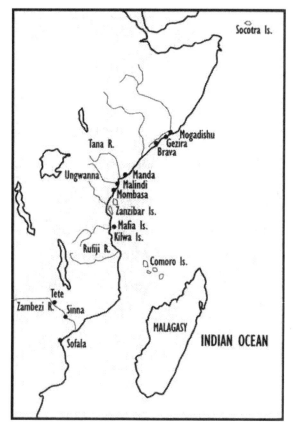

Figure 15. The East African Coast.

Figure 16. 1882 image of the twelfth century Fakhr Al-Din Mosque in Mogadishu.

in the Indian Ocean trade. It was because of the merchant sailors that influences between Africa and Asia spread. The East African ships were mentioned as early as the first century AD in a sailor's guidebook. East African mariners sailed to Oman, India, Java, China, and Cambodia spreading and picking up cultural influences.

The main trading product that the East Africans sold was steel. East Africans had been making this product for nearly 2,000 years. In 1978, thirteen ancient iron furnaces were discovered in Tanzania. These East African smelters made the finest steel produced anywhere in the world before the mid 1800s. The East African cities minted their own coins of copper and silver. The first coins were issued in the eleventh century. They had rhyming couplets on them praising the king and praising God.

The graveyards and mosques were the focal points around which the East African cities grew. The graveyards consisted of Pillar Tombs. They look like little houses with central pillars rising from them. Since the East African coast has around 50 sets of pillar tombs, scholars deduced that perhaps 50 cities and towns flourished along the East African coast from Somalia to Mozambique (one source says 400 settlements). Mogadishu is an example of one of these East African cities. Chinese documents from the fifteenth century mention that Mogadishu had four or five-storey buildings. The houses were made of coral stone.

Figure 17. This article in the *Daily Mail* may be evidence that Swahili sailors from Kilwa reached the Northern Territories of Australia 900 years ago.

Ibn Battuta, a Moroccan visitor, left a description of what he saw in Tanzania in 1331. He wrote the following: "Kilwa is one of the most beautiful and well constructed cities in the world. The whole of it is elegantly built." The Great Mosque of Kilwa is one of the largest surviving Swahili monuments. It was founded in the tenth or eleventh centuries, and enlarged in the thirteenth and fifteenth centuries. The roof was a complicated construction of barrels and domes. Supporting the walls were large triangular buttresses to support such a heavy roof. The interior has a forest of octagonal columns made of rubble and cut stone, set in mortar. One early Portuguese visitor compared its ceiling to that of the Great Mosque of Cordova.

The Royal Palace at Gedi on the coast of Kenya has been much excavated. Archaeologists found evidence of storerooms, kitchens, bedrooms, bathrooms and toilets. I explored this building and counted 54 rooms, 11 courtyards, 7 burial areas and 6 double cubical toilets. Also on the site, were many houses, mosques, and a public water fountain. One curious building was called the House of the Cisterns. This might have been a swimming pool. Another curious building was the House of the Cowries. This might have been a bank.

Figure 18. The Great Mosque of Gedi, thirteenth century AD.

The Ancient and Medieval Nile Valley

So far, I have presented information on West African civilisations before the Slave Trade. I have also presented information on a Central Saharan Empire, a South African Empire, and an East African Confederation. These cultures began well before the slave trade and were many hundreds of years old. I shall now talk about civilisations in Africa that go back many thousands of years as opposed to just hundreds of years.

The Nile Valley was the setting for some of Africa's oldest history. Ancient Nubia (also called the Kingdom of Ta-Seti) consisted of the southern quarter of modern Egypt and the northern half of modern Sudan. On 1 March 1979, the *New York Times* carried an article on page 1 and page 16 called *Nubian Monarchy Called Oldest.* The article concerned archaeological discoveries at Nubian graveyards where a series of royal tombs were found and 5,000 artefacts. The following year *Archaeology Magazine* published a follow-up article entitled *Lost Pharaohs of Nubia.* The archaeologists had found a dynasty of between nine and eleven pharaohs of Nubia who ruled before Egypt's first pharaoh.

Ancient Egypt was Africa's second kingship.

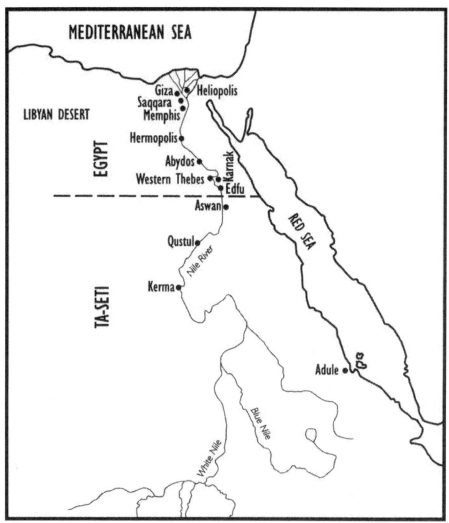

Figure 19. The Ancient Nile Valley.

Physical anthropology has told us a number of things about the Ancient Egyptians. We know they had the same type of hair as Africans do today. Melanin studies conducted on mummies show they had the same complexions as Africans have today. Analysis of mummies and skeletons show they have the same lanky body shape as Africans do today. In addition, genetic studies show the Ancient Egyptians were closely related to the Black Berbers of Morocco and the Pygmies of Central Africa.

We should, of course, remember that the modern people of Egypt are not the same people as the Ancient Egyptians. The modern Arab Egyptians

Figure 20. Pharaoh Mena, the first ruler of Egypt.

conquered Egypt from Arabia in early medieval times (i.e. from December 639 AD onwards). They have continued to dominate and rule North Africa right up to the present time.

Pharaoh Mena was the first ruler of a unified Egypt (Figure 20). There is a portrait head of him in the Petrie Museum, University College London, catalogue number UC 15989. He would appear to be a possible ancestor of Mr Mike Tyson!

The dating of the king is a controversial question. An Ancient Egyptian historian called Manetho dated the beginning of Mena's reign to 5717 BC, which is nearly 8,000 years ago. Other scholars prefer the Berlin Chronology begun by Eduard Meyer, which places Mena at about 3180 BC or just over 5,000 years ago. Some writers, such as Champollion-Figeac, MacNaughton, Pochan and I, have produced timelines that are close to the Manetho dating. Other scholars such as Breasted, Brunson and Rashidi have produced timelines that are close to the Meyer dating.

	DYNASTIES (Dates are BC)			
	I	VI	XII	XVIII
Manetho (3rd century BC)	5717	4426	3440	1674
Wilkinson (1836)	2320			1575
Champollion-Figeac (1839)	5867	4426	3703	1822
Lepsius (1858)	3892	2744	2380	1591
Brugsch (1877)	4400	3300	2466	1700
Meyer (1887)	3180	2530	2130	1530
Breasted (1906)	3400	2625	2000	1580
Petrie (1906)	5510	4206	3459	1580
Petrie (1929)	4553	3282	2586	1587
MacNaughton (1932)	5776	4360	3389	1709
Pochan (1971)	5619	4326	3336	1595
Brunson & Rashidi (1989)	3200	2345	1991	1560
Rohl (1998)	2789	2224	1800	1193
Chinweizu (1999)	4443	3162	1994	1788
Author (2006)	*5660*	*4402*	*3405*	*1709*

On my calculations, Mena ruled from 5660 BC. The time from Dynasty I to Dynasty VI represents Egypt's first golden age. This is called the Old Kingdom Period. Over this time, a total of 50 kings ruled for an astonishing 1,472 years on my calculations (i.e. 5660 to 4188 BC).

During this period, the greatest achievement of the Egyptians was the Pyramid Age. The Great Pyramid of Giza is 481 feet high, with four sides 755 feet each. Mathematicians, scientists, engineers, and astronomers have studied and surveyed this building. All regard this as the most astonishing construction in human history.

Egypt during the Pyramid Age was highly urbanised with cities, towns and ports dotted along the Nile River. Scholars estimate the population of Egypt during this time as 8 million people. Since only the Nile area is habitable, the total area available for habitation was about the size of Belgium. This would make Egypt as urbanised THEN as modern European civilisations are TODAY. Typical one-storey houses from the time had three rooms and a veranda. Typical two-storey houses had six rooms with an outside staircase. Most houses had flat roofs, but some had domed and barrel roofs. Most houses had damp coursing.

In Nubia to the south of Egypt, there was a second golden age centred on the city of Kerma. The city of Kerma covered 65 acres and was surrounded by walls 30 feet high. In the centre of the city was a large white temple.

Figure 21. A panorama of the great Hypostyle Hall at Karnak. (Photo: Blalonde).

Kerma was the most powerful city of the south dominating 242 towns, cities, and districts. In their tombs, archaeologists found exquisite wooden beds. Each of the four legs was shaped like cattle hoofs. The headboards were decorated with images of animals made of inlaid ivory.

The Middle Kingdom was the second golden age of Ancient Egypt. This time period concerns the rulers of Dynasty XI and Dynasty XII. On my calculations, this is a total of 11 kings ruling over 293 years (i.e. 3448 to 3182 BC).

The greatest achievement of this period was the building of the Labyrinth. This building had 3,000 apartments of which 1,500 were below ground and 1,500 were above ground. One of the Greek historians described it as more impressive than all of the great building works of the Greeks combined.

The New Kingdom was the third golden age of Ancient Egypt. This time period concerns the rulers of Dynasties XVIII, XIX and XX. This produced a total of 31 kings ruling for 614 years based on my calculations (i.e. 1709 to 1095 BC).

The greatest achievement of the New Kingdom Egyptians was the Temple Complex of Karnak and Luxor in the city of Waset. This complex was a place of business and culture much like an abbey. Treasures of the ancient world passed through its corridors - gold and precious woods from Sudan, tribute from Syria, and vases from Crete.

The Hypostyle Hall of the Temple of Amen was its greatest structure (Figure 21). It had 134 columns spread out over 56,000 square feet. It was the largest temple of its kind in Ancient Egypt. One could easily fit several European cathedrals into this temple alone. Various architects have commented on this temple. One of them said: "the beauty and massiveness of the forms, and the brilliancy of their coloured decorations, all combine to stamp this as the greatest of man's architectural works." Outside of the Temple were a series of sphinxes representing Aries the Ram. They lined both sides of the walkway leading to the Temple. If one follows the line of sphinxes it takes us all the way from Karnak to the Temple of Amen in

Luxor. The whole city of Waset had a circumference of nine miles and housed one million people.

In 860 BC, the land to the south enjoyed a third a golden age that lasted until 350 AD. The southern land was now called Kush. Nuri was its first capital city. It was a city of pyramids. The Nuri pyramids were the oldest of the 223 Kushite pyramids. The early rulers of Kush were buried at this site.

Pharaoh Taharqo was the most powerful of the Kushite rulers. He ruled from 690 to 664 BC. Unlike previous rulers who called themselves 'Lords of Kush' or 'Lords of the Two Lands,' he considered himself the Emperor of the World. He ruled a vast empire including Kush, Egypt, North Africa, Syria, and Spain. Even the city of Carthage in North Africa was within his sphere of influence. The city of Napata became the second capital of Kush during his time. Taharqo completed a great monument there called the Temple of Amen. It was 150 metres long and the most important religious building in Kush. He also built a monument dedicated to the deity Bes (Figure 22).

The Kushite rulers placed their female relatives on the thrones of Egypt. Chief Prophetess of Amen, Shepenoupet II, was one such ruler. She was the last independent black ruler of Egypt. The Assyrians from the Middle East seized Egypt from Kush in 663 BC and had her deposed. Kush was now only a country and not an empire, having lost control of Egypt.

From this date until today, Egypt has never been free of foreign control. After being ruled by the Assyrians, Egypt was colonised by the Persians, then the Greeks, the Romans and finally, the Arabs. This is why the modern Egyptians are no longer Africans. They are a mixture of the various peoples that have occupied Egypt since the time of Shepenoupet II.

In the fourth century BC, the Kushites invented a new script called Meroïtic. There are 900 surviving documents in this script. Some of these documents are stone inscriptions others were written on papyri. The script was made up of 23 letters including four vowels and a word divider. The Kushites also invented a numerical system for mathematics. They achieved much higher levels of public literacy than the Egyptians ever did.

The city of Meroë became the last capital of Kush. The rulers were buried there from 250 BC to 350 AD. There were 84 pyramids in Meroë, each with their own chapels. The pyramids were 20 to 30 metres high and slope at 70° (Figure 24). Sir E. A. Wallis Budge wrote a two-volume book called *The Egyptian Sudan.* In this book, he had images of these pyramids with captions such as: "The Queen of Meroë who built Pyramid No. 11, and her

Figure 22. The Temple of Bes in Napata, seventh century BC.

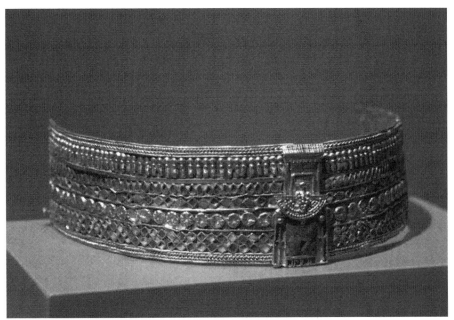
Figure 23. Golden jewellery of Amanishakheto. (Photo: Sven-Steffen Arndt).

Figure 24. Aerial view of the Pyramids at Meroë. (Photo: B. N. Chagny).

consort." Another example is: "The Queen of Meroë who built Pyramid No.6 spearing captives." Sir Budge is raising the question of to what extent the Kushite civilisation was dominated by women.

The Pyramid of Queen Mother Amanishakheto has attracted curious interest. When it was discovered in the early 1800s, it was still intact. Unfortunately, an Italian grave robber destroyed it in 1834. Inside, he found golden armlets, signet rings, shield rings, and jewellery of all kinds made of gold and inlaid glass. These golden artefacts are now called the Treasures of Amanishakheto (Figure 23). Gold was a most important Kushite product. Herodotus, the ancient Greek historian, claimed gold was so plentiful that it was used to enchain prisoners! This seemed unlikely until archaeologists discovered that the Kushites even had golden tweezers!

Pharaoh Arnekhamani ruled from 235 to 221 BC. During his time, great monuments were built at Musawarat. The Temple of Apedemak is still standing and in a good state of repair. The Temple Complex at Musawarat was the largest in old Kush. It was a massive and ambitious temple complex that linked at least four temples together with walls and corridors. It may originally have been a pilgrimage site. However, a new theory claims that this building was a university. It had walls and statues covered with gold leaf.

Before leaving Kush, it is worth pointing out that archaeologists have found delicate glass vases made by the Kushites. They were made of blue glass with golden images and writing. They made these delightful artefacts between 250 and 300 AD.

After Kush fell in 350 AD, three Nubian kingdoms replaced it (Figure 25). Creating a fourth golden age in the south, Nobadia was the most northerly of the kingdoms, Makuria was in the middle, and Alwa was in the south. However, by the seventh century Nobadia and Makuria fused into a single empire. There were thus two Nubian kingdoms, Makuria and Alwa. This medieval golden age takes us from 350 AD to 1500 AD.

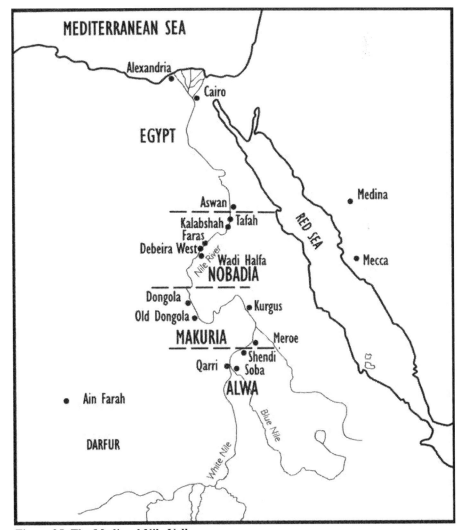

Figure 25. The Medieval Nile Valley.

A number of elegant silver crowns decorated with rubies were found buried with Nubian dignitaries dating to the fourth century. These crowns were similar to ones worn by the princes and viceroys of Kush and probably indicate that the medieval Nubians considered themselves descendants of Kush.

The three Nubian kingdoms became Christian in the sixth century. They built a number of churches and cathedrals. The typical Nubian church was built on a basilica plan with three or five aisles. Hundreds of village and small town churches were built on the basilica plan.

In the seventh century, the Nubians built the Cathedral of Granite Columns in the Makurian capital of Old Dongola. This was probably the most important religious building in Makuria. In 707 AD, they built the Cathedral of Faras. This was probably the most important religious building in Nobadia.

Figure 26. *Miracles of St Menas*, 1053 AD.

Another important Nobadian monument was the Cathedral at Qasr Ibrim. Originally dedicated to Our Lady the Pure Virgin Mary, it had a high dome and cross. Arab invaders ransacked and burned the building in 956 but archaeologists in 1969 rediscovered the Cathedral's archives. The archives contained thousands of documents of a legal or ecclesiastical nature. There were found to be in many different languages such as Old Nubian, Meroïtic, Coptic, Arabic, Turkish, Latin, Greek, and Greek Creole. Clearly, the archivists could read and write in many different languages!

Incidentally, I saw a 1053 AD Nubian manuscript on display at a Byzantium exhibition in Central London entitled *Miracles of St Menas* (Figure 26).

The Emperors of Makuria ruled from the Throne Hall of Old Dongola. Built in the ninth or tenth centuries, it was a two-storey building decorated with murals with walls 1.1 metres thick. The Emperor ruled as king of 13 Makuria kings. Old Dongola itself was excavated by the Polish archaeologists who found eighth and ninth century housing complexes with bathrooms that possessed water supply installations and heating systems!

Things however eventually fell apart. The Makurian Empire faced many invasions from the Arabs in 1276, 1304, 1316 and 1365. Kulubnarti Castle was the last stronghold of the Nubians before they were eventually overrun. Bring the story up to date, the Arabs are still battling Africans in Darfur, Southern Sudan, and in Mauritania.

Ancient and Medieval Ethiopia

Ancient Ethiopia has thousands of years of history stretching from the ancient period through the medieval period. It also shared a lot of history with Yemen across the Red Sea (Figure 27).

The city of Axum was an early capital of Ethiopia. It has a series of seven gigantic stelae made of granite and dedicated to the moon deity, Mahrem. They built these obelisks between 300 BC and AD 300. The largest standing stele has details of a nine-storey building carved into it and weighs an astonishing 300 tons. It must be understood that your car weighs two thirds of a ton therefore 300 tons is the same weight as 450 cars.

What is interesting is that the standing obelisk is not the largest one they ever built. There is a monument in Axum known as the Fallen Obelisk. This is the largest such obelisk in the world. It has details of a thirteen-storey building carved into it and weighs 500 tons. This may be the equivalent of 650 cars in weight. It has since fallen over but no one can move it!

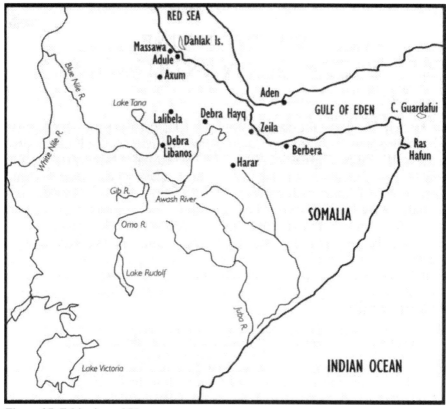

Figure 27. Ethiopia and Yemen.

Coins were minted in Axum. They were made of gold, silver, or bronze. Only four nations at that time could issue in gold - Rome, Persia, the Kushan Kingdom of India, and Ethiopia. The coins name over 20 early rulers of Ethiopia (Figure 28). The Ethiopians traded with Kush, Egypt, the Roman Empire, Arabia, India, and China. In around 330 AD, Ethiopia became Christian. To celebrate this they built the Cathedral of St Mary of Zion, one of the oldest Christian cathedrals on earth. They also issued coins with the Christian cross on them and the motto: "May the country be satisfied!"

Just as there are old manuscripts in West Africa, there are old manuscripts in Ethiopia. Professor Richard Pankhurst, a famous Ethiopianist, estimates that 250,000 old manuscripts are still around. Scholars have microfiched 12,000 of them. The oldest one has recently been redated to before 650 AD (Figure 29). Many of these old illuminated manuscripts are held in

Figure 28. Coin of the Axumite ruler Ousas. (Photo: Classical Numismatic Group, Inc.)

Ethiopian churches and monasteries. Ethiopia also has an impressive tradition of paintings, mostly of religious scenes. A particularly famous scene is a painting called *Our Lady of Debra Metmaq*. Everybody in the scene is painted red, has an afro, and is looking to the side. The colour red has symbolic value in many traditions of African art. What is really interesting here is that Our Lady is portrayed with a red, green and gold halo. Also depicted are three saints, St Theodore with his red horse, St Mercurios with his black horse, and St George with his white horse. This is the same St George that we know and love in the UK! In this painting, he is given an afro just like everybody else!

The city of Roha became the capital during the time of Emperor Lalibela (*c.*1150-1220 AD). The city contains eleven churches that were carved out on the ground by hammer and chisel! The House of the Redeemer of the World is the largest is of these monuments. It is an impressive 33.7 metres long, 23.7 metres wide and 11.5 metres deep. The base is the only thing that connects it to the rock from which it was carved. The House of Mary was next door. It is 15 metres long, 11 metres wide and 10 metres deep. Outside of this building was a baptismal pool. Emperor Lalibela, himself, considered this his favourite and held the mass at this church. The House of Emmanuel is another famous church.

The British Museum scholar, Sir E. A. Wallis Budge, was the first is to proclaim Lalibela as the Eighth Wonder of the World. At the present time, the Ethiopian Tourist Commission markets this city in this way.

Top: Figure 29. *Daily Telegraph* article with new data on Ethiopian manuscripts.
Bottom: Figure 30. Church of St George, Lalibela. (Photo: Bernard Gagnon).

Figure 31. Another view of the Church of St George, Lalibela. (Photo: Bernard Gagnon).

Conclusion

When we bring together the history of Black people, we see that that history has much to be proud of. It is not just a history of being a slave.

The Grand Mosque of Djenné is the largest clay brick building on earth. The city of Timbuktu had a university where 700,000 of its old manuscripts are still held by black families and institutions. The rulers of the region were rumoured to be the richest men on the face of the earth. One of them, Mansa Musa I, is the richest man in all human history. Benin City is in the *Guinness Book of Records* as the largest earthworks in the world. Benin art was the finest metal art of the Middle Ages. In Kanem-Borno, it was possible to cash a cheque. In Munhumutapa, the gold miners dug 43 1/4 million tons of ore. One scholar has estimated that this would produce pure gold to the value of $7.5 billion in 1998 money. The Tanzanian city of Kilwa was considered one of the most beautiful cities in the world. The new discoveries in Ancient Nubia have shown that kingship originated in Africa. The Ancient Egyptians built the Great Pyramid of Giza and the Temple Complex of Karnak and Luxor, the greatest achievements in the

Figure 32. Museum of African Art, Jeju-do, South Korea. The design was based on the Great Mosque of Djenné (Figure 5).

architectural history of the human race. In Kush, archaeologists have counted 223 pyramids. They have also discovered golden tweezers! In Medieval Nubia, archaeologists found housing complexes with bathrooms and heating systems, not to mention archives with documents in eight different languages. Ethiopia has the largest sculpted obelisk ever built. Ethiopia also has the Eighth Wonder of the World - a city of underground churches.

I give the final word to Professor Charles Seifert, an African-American scholar. He wrote an unusual booklet in 1938 called *The Negro's or Ethiopian's Contribution to Art.* He began the booklet with a statement that brilliantly explains why it is import to know your history: "To all Ethiopians--Black men at home and abroad who desire to live on equality with all men: Know the truth and the truth will make you free. Then, take your place in the ranks of all men--Brown, Yellow, White and Black. This is your God-given Right. Nothing more, nothing less. A Race without the knowledge of its history is like a tree without roots. It is the inspiring influence of that knowledge which makes men want to go forward. The whole future of man is bound up in the doings of the past. Know it well and no one will be able to deceive or make you afraid. Your historic records prove that you are the greatest benefactors of the whole human race; this knowledge should encourage you and cause you to put the mighty force within you to work. Then no man will have need to call you to labour. Come! Beloved, take up your cross, take your place in the ranks once more, you are delaying the caravan."

FOR FURTHER READING ON AFRICAN HISTORY

1. The Songhai Empire

The account of the Songhai Empire presented here was accurate but highly simplified. Songhai was actually the third of three vast empires to rule over West Africa in former times. All three empires were approximately in the same area. Consequently, a few of the achievements that I presented as 'Songhai' were actually achieved during the dominance of the earlier two empires.

The first of these empires was Ancient Ghana. Beginning as a small kingdom in around 300 AD, Ancient Ghana came to rule half of West Arica as an empire from around 700 AD until 1240 AD. The second of these empires was Mediaeval Mali. Beginning as a vassal kingdom of Ancient Ghana in around 800 AD, the Malians conquered Ghana, their former

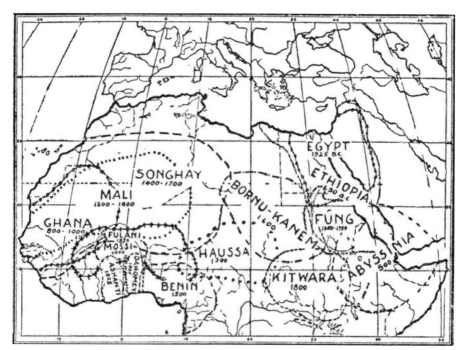

Figure 33. The empires of Ancient Ghana, Mali and Songhai at the height of their power in the eleventh, fourteenth and sixteenth centuries respectively.

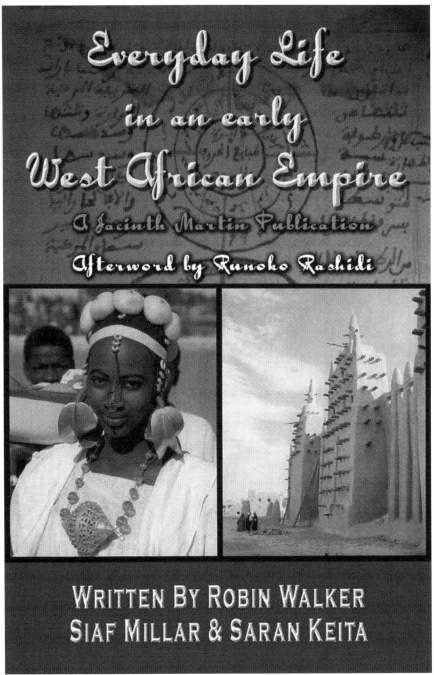

Figure 34. The most advanced book on the Songhai Empire is *Everyday Life in an early West African Empire* available from
www.everydaylifeinanearlywestafricanempire.com

rulers, in 1240. After this, they ruled an empire that dominated West Africa from the early 1300s until 1433. Songhai began as a kingdom in around 690 AD and had two empire periods. The first empire was in the early 1000s and lasted until conquered by Mali in 1325. The second empire began after 1464 and lasted until 1591. At its height the Songhai ruled two thirds of West Africa.

How do these facts alter the presentation of the history? I presented Timbuktu as the cultural capital of the Songhai Empire. This was certainly true of the period 1469 to 1591. However, Timbuktu is known to have been founded by desert nomads in around 1100 AD. This meant that Timbuktu began as a Ghana Empire settlement. The city also existed during the dominance of the Empire of Mediaeval Mali. But there is more. Archaeologists claim that earlier sites dating from 400 or 500 AD may have been the parents of Timbuktu. Even though Ancient Ghana was a kingdom from around 300 AD, it probably did not come to rule the Timbuktu region until around 700 AD.

Consequently, Timbuktu's history, from a local's perspective would look like this. In perhaps 400 or 500 AD, locals established two relevant settlements. We do not know the name of each settlement but modern archaeologists call one of these 'Tombouze' and they call the other one 'Wadi el-Ahmar'. In around 700 AD the region was conquered by the rulers of Ancient Ghana. These two settlements became Ghanaian cities. During the height of Ghanaian power, desert nomads established a new settlement in around 1100 called Timbuktu very close to Tombouze and Wadi el-Ahmar. The new settlement eventually absorbed the older settlements. In the 1300s, Timbuktu became a Malian city as Mali came to dominate more than half of all West Africa. Finally Timbuktu was absorbed into the second Songhai Empire in 1469 and remained a Songhai city until the fall of Songhai after 1591.

What do we know about the history of this region? Lady Lugard, an English journalist, wrote the first important modern book on these three empires. Her book, *A Tropical Dependency* (UK, James Nisbet & Co., 1905) has recently been made available by other publishers. Many of the larger and older libraries may also have this book.

As brilliant as this work was, however, it contains some major errors of fact and interpretation. More importantly, it has a marked anti-Negro tone that runs through the book. In fact, the majority of late nineteenth and early twentieth century works on African history by European scholars suffer from this problem. I believe the book, like all the others mentioned here, is still worth reading but the reader should be aware of the problems they may encounter.

Professor J. Spencer Trimingham wrote a book called *A History of Islam in West Africa* (UK, Oxford University Press, 1962). Containing excellent chapters on Ghana, Mali, Songhai, and Kanem-Borno, the book quotes directly from primary written documents. Moreover, the book maintains a respectful tone throughout towards Africans.

I have written a useful account of Ghana, Mali and Songhai history in *When We Ruled*, Chapter 12 (UK, Reklaw Education, 2013, pp.424-463). I have also co-written *Everyday Life in an early West African Empire* with Siaf Millar and Saran Keita (UK, SIVEN, 2013). This book is the most detailed study of the Songhai Empire written to date.

2. Great Benin

The classic study of Great Benin was the book by English scholar Henry Ling Roth, *Great Benin, Its Customs, Art and Horrors* (UK, F. King and Sons, 1903). Written from the accounts of diplomats, explorers and envoys to Benin, the book gives an outsider's perspective of Benin history.

Chief Jacob Egharevba's book, *A Short History of Benin* (Nigeria, Ibadan University Press, 1968), was written using the surviving oral traditions on each king from around 900 AD to the fall of Benin in 1897. This book gives an insider's perspective on Benin history by an indigenous Nigerian scholar.

I wrote an account of Benin history that combined the written documents with the surviving oral traditions in *When We Ruled*, Chapter 11 (UK, Reklaw Education, 2013, pp.392-405).

3. The Kanem-Borno Empire

The classic study of Kanem-Borno was the work by the English scholar Sir Herbert Richmond Palmer, *The Bornu Sahara and Sudan* (UK, John Murray, 1936). A work of breathtakingly learned scholarship, it is very difficult to read. Moreover, Palmer does not resolve the differences and contradictions between the oral traditions and the written documentation into a single coherent story.

I wrote a useful account of Kanem-Borno in *When We Ruled*, Chapter 14 (UK, Reklaw Education, 2013, pp.492-505).

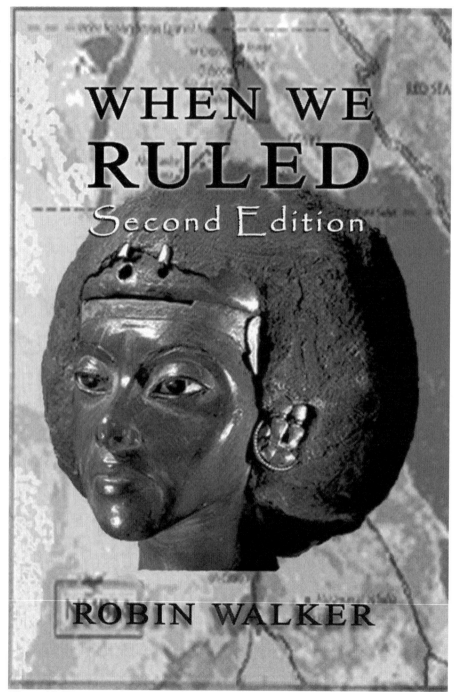

Figure 35. The most advanced book on general early African history is *When We Ruled* available from www.whenweruled.com

4. The Munhumutapa Empire

Scholarship on the Munhumutapa Empire has always remained controversial. Earlier European writers formed into two camps to write the history of the region.

J. Theodore Bent wrote *The Ruined Cities of Mashonaland* (UK, Longmans, Green & Co, 1892). Representative of one of the two camps, he described the Southern African civilisation as a high and literate culture of great antiquity. Bent, however, claimed that Black Africans had nothing to do with the building of this civilisation! Instead, he claims that mysterious visitors from the Middle East built this civilisation.

Dr David Randall McIver wrote *Mediaeval Rhodesia* (UK, Macmillan and Co., 1906). Representative of other of the two camps, McIver correctly described the Southern African culture as wholly African. However, there was a catch. He presents Munhumutapa as a low and illiterate culture of only mediaeval age!

I wrote an account of Munhumutapa that draws from the best of both camps in the light of the recent archaeology in *When We Ruled,* Chapter 17 (UK, Reklaw Education, 2013, pp.592-621).

5. The Swahili Confederation

The pioneering study of the East African coastal culture was the book by British colonial administrator Captain Stigand entitled *The Land of Zinj* (UK, Constable & Company, 1913). A most imperfect work, the author manages to trace everything of importance in the Swahili Civilisation to Arabian or Persian origins.

Fortunately, Dr Basil Davidson, an important and influential English scholar corrected this misinformation in *Old Africa Rediscovered* (UK, Victor Gollancz, 1959). A work of profound implications, Davidson also dismissed the racist ideas that Ancient Ghana had white origins, Benin had Roman origins, Kanem-Borno had mysterious origins, and Munhumutapa had Middle Eastern origins.

I wrote an account of the Swahili Confederation that draws from the best of the evidence in the light of the recent archaeology in *When We Ruled,* Chapter 15 (UK, Reklaw Education, 2013, pp.542-554).

6. The Ancient and Medieval Nile Valley

The history of Black people in the Nile Valley civilisations remains the most controversial and acrimonious topic area in African history. It is even possible that this topic will remain a divisive issue for the next fifty years.

Professor Cheikh Anta Diop, the famous Senegalese scholar, wrote *The African Origin of Civilization: Myth or Reality?* (US, Lawrence Hill Books, 1974). It is the classic book to argue that the Ancient Egyptians were in fact Black Africans. I have updated some of his arguments as new evidence has become available in *When We Ruled,* Chapter 9 (UK, Reklaw Education, 2013, pp.317-347).

Duncan MacNaughton wrote the classic book that challenged the 'short' Berlin Chronology of Ancient Egyptian dating. He advocated for the 'long' chronology instead. His book was entitled *A Scheme of Egyptian Chronology* (UK, Luzac & Co., 1932). I have updated some of his arguments as new evidence has become available in *When We Ruled,* Chapter 8 (UK, Reklaw Education, 2013, pp.277-316).

Most of what we know about The Kingdom of Ta-Seti and the city of Kerma comes from relatively recent archaeological excavations. On the other hand, most of Egypt's ancient history was well known to the historians from the late 1800s. I wrote an account that combines the Sudanese and Egyptian Pharaonic history that draws from the best of the evidence in the light of recent archaeology in *When We Ruled,* Chapters 6 and 7 (UK, Reklaw Education, 2013, pp.175-276).

One of the first substantial books on the mediaeval history of Nubia was *Churches in Lower Nubia* by English architect G. S. Mileham (US, University of Philadelphia, 1910).

I wrote an account of Mediaeval Nubia that combines the best of the evidence in the light of the recent archaeology in *When We Ruled,* Chapter 16 (UK, Reklaw Education, 2013, pp.559-591).

7. Ancient and Medieval Ethiopia

The pioneering study of Ethiopian history in the English language is Sir E. A. Wallis Budge's *A History of Ethiopia, Nubia & Abyssinia* (UK, John Murray, 1928). It is a good piece of scholarship but, again, suffers from all the anti-Negro hatreds and biases typical of European scholarship from that period. Budge manages to attribute everything of value in Ethiopian culture to outside influences!

I wrote an account of Ethiopian history that draws from a wide range of evidence in *When We Ruled,* Chapter 15 (UK, Reklaw Education, 2013, pp.526-541).

Figure 36. This study guide will help you read, understand and master *When We Ruled* in 60 days. It is available from www.amazon.com

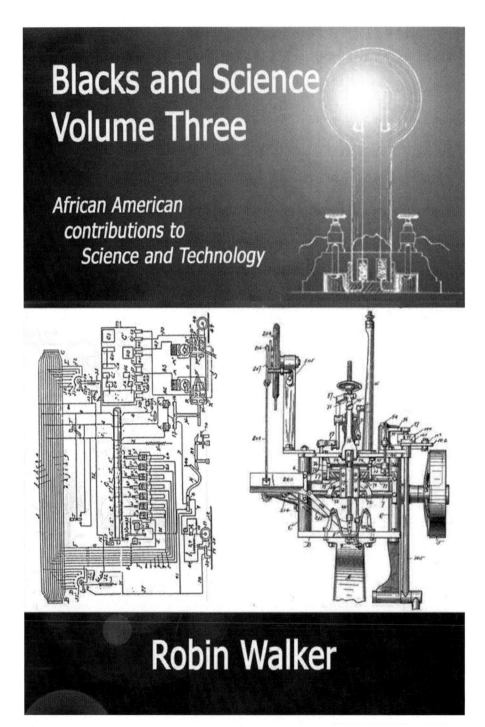

Figure 37. This book is available from www.amazon.com

PART TWO

50 QUESTIONS & ANSWERS ABOUT THE HISTORY OF BLACK PEOPLE

INTRODUCTION

In putting this part of the book together, I wanted to address the 50 most commonly asked questions that Black people have on Black history that have not been properly addressed … until now!

All questions in this book have been asked by Black members of the British and American public. In turn each question has been answered by me, a Black history expert based in London.

This part of the book is designed to help you develop a good degree of knowledge about Black history. I aim to do two things for you:

* Learn Black history quickly
* Skyrocket your self confidence

Enjoy and learn!

Robin Walker

50 QUESTIONS & ANSWERS ABOUT THE HISTORY OF BLACK PEOPLE

1. Did every race come from Black people?

Every race of people came from Black people. The evidence comes from the recent research completed on something called mitochondrial DNA. The pioneer of that type of study is Professor Rebecca Cann from the

Figure 38. From the *Daily Mail*, 11 May 1995.

University of Berkley. She showed that all human beings can be traced back to a parent population using mitochondrial DNA. In addition, that parent population can be traced back to Africa. Her article was called 'Mitochondrial DNA and Human Evolution' which was published in 1987 in *Nature* magazine. The same evidence was dumbed down and published in *Newsweek*. The information was dumbed down further and appeared in the *Daily Mail*. It is now the generally accepted theory.

However, some of the scholars who popularized the theory called the African ancestor 'Mitochondrial Eve.' Other scholars have said that 'Eve' is not an appropriate term, as they feel that this is sneaking in *The Bible* through the back door. No early African ancestor is likely to have been called 'Eve' as this is a Jewish and not an African name.

There is more information on this topic in my book *When We Ruled,* Chapter 5 (UK, Reklaw Education, 2013, pp.157-166).

2. Where did White people come from: the Caucasus Mountains?

White people have the same mitochondrial DNA connection as all other peoples. This link ultimately connects them to a distant African ancestry.
However, Europeans have had a belief for some time that their more recent ancestors originated in the Caucasus Mountains (of the Turkey/Southern Russia region). Consequently when scholars in the 18th century came up with a name for the White race, they called them 'Caucasians'.

Professor Charles Finch, an African American scholar, wrote a book called *Echoes of the Old Darkland.* In this book he develops this idea and gives it a scholarly make over. He believes that the early African ancestors that migrated to the Caucasus region evolved into Caucasians. The only problem here is that while Finch himself believes that the earliest evidence of Caucasian skeletons will be found in the Caucasus Mountains, at the time of writing his book (which was 1991) the evidence hadn't yet been found. It still has not been found.

The oldest evidence that I am aware of is that White people evolved in the region of southern France. In the lowest strata that archaeologists have dug up (about 39,000 years ago), they found African type skeletons often showing evidence of vitamin D deficiency which causes deformities like rickets. However, in the more recent strata of the same cave areas (about 20,000 years ago); they found skeletons that didn't suffer from vitamin D deficiency. These skeletons also had cranial shapes more in line with European cranial shapes.

Many scholars, including Professor Diop (see question 23), regard this as evidence of the evolution of the European race from African ancestors, but in southern France.

3. Why do certain ancient Egyptian corpses have Caucasian hair?

It is true that many surviving ancient Egyptian mummies have hair that appears to be straight (as opposed to woolly), and blonde or red (as opposed to black). But it is very unwise to jump to hasty conclusions.

Archaeologists are trained from a book called *Science and Archaeology* by two scholars, Don Brothwell and Eric Higgs. In this book is an essay called the 'The Hair of the Earlier Peoples', which is a guide for archaeologists in how to interpret ancient hair.

A two hundred year old mummy found in Malawi had what appeared to be dark brown hair! This raises the question: Why dark brown and not black? This demonstrates what happens to dead African hair after just two hundred years. When we go to the ancient Egyptian period we are talking two and a half thousand years and beyond. So hair that starts off as black, can turn brown and then blonde.

The essay went on to give examples of hair found in South America where black hair is standard, but some of the buried corpses have what appears to be blonde hair. Burials from the Canary Islands where everyone has black hair, some of them have also turned blonde. This is what happens to dead hair over many hundred of years.

As far as ancient Egyptian hair coming out straight, the mummification process can result in a number of ways in which hair can be damaged and, according to the essay, the damage can result in a permanent wave. Permanent waving (or a 'perm') results in Black people's hair coming out straight. Moreover, the same thing has been observed in sheep's wool. The essay does not say why they gave sheep's wool as an example, but I believe they chose sheep's wool because it is the closest to African hair!

The essay gives various theories of the sort of damage to ancient Egyptian hair that could cause an effect similar to permanent waving, such as atmospheric weathering, alkaline soil, things caused by the embalming process, and the lack of care to the hair over the subsequent two or three thousand years.

There is more information on this topic in my book *When We Ruled*, Chapter 9 (UK, Reklaw Education, 2013, pp.330-331).

4. Did Black people enslave each other before slavery?

Yes they did.

Slavery existed across the world and was practised by nearly all civilisations including European ones and African ones. Slavery did not have a colour and consequently the various civilisations had slaves of their own race. The reason why civilisations had slaves was the same as why modern nations jail individuals: i.e. as punishment for debt or as punishment for committing a crime.

Slaves in African civilisations performed various roles from plantation workers, domestic servants, policeman and guards, members of the government or even administrative staff. In exceptional situations they rose from slave to emperor.

It is important not to confuse slavery in African civilisations or slavery in the ancient world with the type of slavery that Black people experienced in the Western Hemisphere since 1492. This type of slavery was very different in the level of cruelty and brutality.

There is more information on Black people enslaving Black people in my book (co written by Siaf Millar and Saran Keita) *Everyday Life in an early West African Empire,* (UK, SIVEN, 2013, pp.100-103, 105, 108, 118-119).

5. What happened to the original people of the Caribbean before slavery?

The original people of the Caribbean were Native Americans. The native peoples did not have a single name that covered them all but Europeans mistakenly called them 'Indians.' In North America they became known as 'Red Indians.' In the Caribbean they were known by different ethnic groups such as the 'Taino.'

So what happened to these original people?

They were mass murdered by the Spanish in one of the saddest chapters in human history. For example Christopher Columbus estimated that over 1 million people lived in Haiti at the time he arrived in 1492. By the middle of the 16th century this population had been drastically reduced to just 14 individuals.

The level of violence was so bad that a European priest, the Rev Bartolome De Las Casas, wrote a book called *The Tears of the Indians* to persuade his fellow Europeans to stop the violence against the Native Americans.

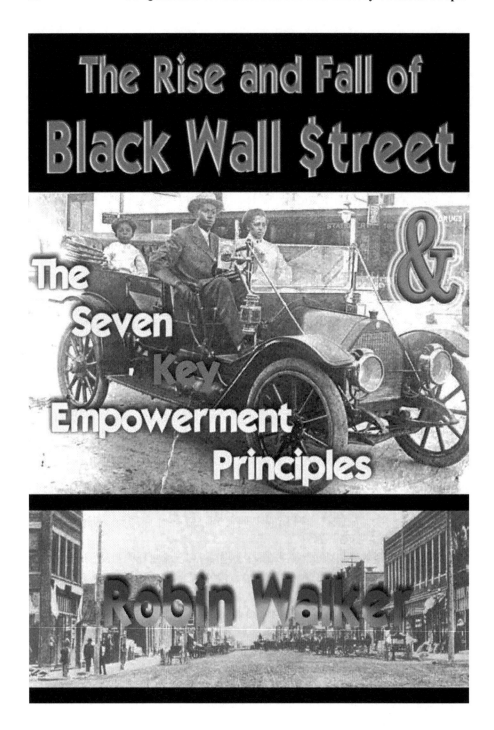

Figure 39. This book is available from www.amazon.com

Figure 40. The Williams Dreamland Theatre was one of the business successes that flourished on Black Wall Street.

6. What was the 'Black Wall Street'?

The 'Black Wall Street' was a black business district in the city of Tulsa, Oklahoma. At its height in 1921, there was a Black population of 11,000 people who had an estimated 600 businesses! Among these were 13 churches, 2 schools, and a hospital. The wealthy Blacks lived in fine homes with linens, china, and grand pianos. It began fashionable to dangle gold pieces (i.e. watches) from chains which became a status symbol.

There are claims that 3 Blacks were millionaires (some say 6) and that some of them even had private planes.

It is interesting to compare what 11,000 Black Tulsans in 1921 could achieve with what 2,000,000 Black Britons today have, which isn't nearly as much.

There is more information on this topic in my book *The Rise and Fall of Black Wall Street & The Seven Key Empowerment Principles,* (UK, Reklaw Education, 2014, pp.1-40).

7. Were the Moors Black?

Many people confuse the Moors with Arabs. Similarly, there is confusion between Black and non-Black Moors.

Figure 41. Moorish gentleman playing chess attended to by Black and white servants from a 13th century Spanish manuscript.

The term Moor is old term for Black people but it has since changed its name, so now when the word is mentioned it is usually used to refer to the modern Moroccans, many of whom are not black.

During medieval times, there were various Moorish dynasties that ruled Spain and Portugal. The first one was known as the Umayyad Dynasty who ruled from 756 to 1031 AD. Its founder was Abd-al-Rahman I, who was of part Moorish and part Yemeni ancestry. Since the Yemenis of this period were black, Abd-al-Rahman I was fully black. The same, however, cannot be said for the rest of his dynasty as intermarriage with blonde women was common. The second ruling dynasty was known as the Almoravides who originated in Senegal, West Africa. The third dynasty was known as the Almohades. They were Black Moroccans from out of the Atlas Mountains. The fourth and final dynasty was an Arab dynasty known as the Nasrids. They started off as an Arab dynasty but through many years of intermarriage, they ended up as black.

There is more information on this topic in my book *When We Ruled,* Chapters 4 and 13 (UK, Reklaw Education, 2013, pp.132-143, 464-488).

8. Were there any Black Anglo-Saxons?

As far as we know the answer is probably no.

The Anglo-Saxons were originally resided in Germany. They entered England after 400 AD in various waves of migration. The word 'Anglo' is coming from the words 'Angle' and 'Angeln'. 'Angeln' is a place name in Germany. 'Saxon' is coming from 'Saxony' which is an old name for Germany. The Angles and Saxons entered England and eventually took over and renamed the country. 'England' is derived from 'Angeln'.

The population of England at the time was largely Celtic. There were also Romans living in England. Among these Romans were Black people from Africa who were part of the Roman Empire. There was even a recent British television documentary about one of these African Romans. She is called the 'Ivory Bangle Woman' and is thought to have been a queen or some other elite individual. She was buried in York in the fourth century AD.

It is interesting to note that Africans were living in Britain before the Anglo-Saxons got here.

9. Did slavery build up the American Wall Street?

Some scholars say yes.

I have heard the African American scholar Anthony T. Browder lecture on this.

He said that Wall Street began as an actual wall. When enslaved people disembarked from the slave ships they could be moved past these walls so that the traders didn't have to look at or face these victims.

10. What were Black people like before slavery?

Just to give one example, we have the description of the West African Empire of Mali given by Ibn Battuta. He wrote in 1353 based on his visit to Mali in 1352. This gives a good picture of West Africa before the Slave Trade began in 1441. The Mali Empire ruled about half of West Africa at the time.

He said that here was complete security in Mali where neither traveller nor inhabitant in it has anything to fear from robbery or men of violence. For someone who has travelled all over the world (as Ibn Battuta had) to say that meant that Mali must have been exceptional!

Ibn Battuta gave the following example: If a white man had died in Mali nobody would touch his goods, they would simply find another white person and ask whether they would like to take the goods.

This would give the impression that the people of Mali were highly spiritual and very moral.

11. What was the first Black newspaper published?

The first Black newspaper was published in the United States. Founded in the early 19th century, it was called the *Freedoms Journal.*

Black abolitionists set up the newspaper to hopefully popularise the idea in America that mass enslavement should be ended. The British abolished the transportation of enslaved people in 1807 and abolished mass enslavement in 1838, but America still had it as late as 1865. This is why it was very important for the Black abolitionists to keep up the fight in America and the *Freedoms Journal* was part of that struggle.

12. Did Black people invent glass?

Over ten yeas ago at the Association for the Study of Classical African Civilizations conference in London, Dr Amon Saba Saakana gave a presentation on the existence of glass in pre dynastic Egypt. This was clearly where glass started.

When I teach or lecture, I like to show ancient Kushite glass artefacts from the Sudanese site of Sedeinga. Among the things found were glass vases made from blue glass decorated with gold writing.

In medieval West Africa, the emperor of Ghana lived in a fortified chateau that had glass windows. This monument was built in 1116 AD.

Finally, many years ago I attended an exhibit at the British Museum based on excavations in the West African city of Gao (in Mali). One of the exhibits on display was fragments of alabaster window surrounds with a piece of window glass. This was from Gao and dated from the 10th to the 14th centuries AD.

13. How and where did Asians come from?

I use the term 'Asian' in the American sense of the term which is a reference to yellow or Mongoloid people, such as the Chinese, Japanese and Koreans.

Some anthropologists say they were the third race to emerge as a mixture of Black and white. The early Black people who emerged from Africa to populate the globe would have been of Pygmy or of Khoisan appearance. Nelson Mandela is perhaps the most famous Khoisan on the planet and he possesses vaguely 'Oriental' features. However, not that he looks 'Oriental', but rather they look like him.

If you could imagine a population of people looking like that and with a small admixture of white, enough to straighten the hair, you can see how the ancient race changed into the yellow (or Mongolian) race. The most reasonable date for the evolution of the Mongolian race would have been about 15,000 years ago. The same stock of people moved from Asia to the Americas, spreading south and becoming the Native Americans.

14. If the ancient Egyptians were Black why are there so many White people in their pictures?

The truth is there aren't many white people in ancient Egyptian pictures. Egyptian art normally depicts some people as red and others the colour yellow. It is perhaps some of the yellow imagery that some people confuse as depicting white people.

Why did they depict individuals as red or yellow?

No one really knows why but we can theorize. However, if you look at ancient Sudanese art, some individuals are painted in red and others are painted in yellow. If we go to the other side of Africa, for example Yoruba art, some individuals are painted red and some are painted yellow. In each

Figure 42. Wall painting from the XX Dynastic Period that shows a prince being embraced by the Goddess Isis. He is shown as red, she is shown as yellow. The yellow images have led to the confusion that these images depict Caucasians.

case it is typically the males shown as red and the females are shown as yellow.

Clearly these colours are colour symbols as no society produces males who are red skinned and females who are yellow skinned. If you look at ancient Greek art you'll see men painted black and women painted white. Does this prove that ancient Greek men were Black? Of course NOT! What it does prove is that we have to use intelligence when we look at ancient art.

So much for the so-called 'Caucasian' imagery.

There is more information on this topic in my book *When We Ruled,* Chapter 9 (UK, Reklaw Education, 2013, pp.333-340).

15. What about the European statues in ancient Egypt?

Many Black people assume that in order to be an unmixed Black you need to have the widest nose with the broadest features i.e. the so called 'True Negro'. However when you look at a group of Black people you will find individuals who look like that but you won't find everyone looking like that.

The point is this: Black people are the oldest people on the planet and therefore have undergone the most evolution compared to any other peoples on the planet. Therefore you'll find Somalians, Kenyans and Ugandans with very narrow facial features. In addition, there are West Africans in the desert areas such as the Malians and some of the Hausas of Nigeria with very narrow features. Since they are darker than everyone else no one can claim them to have been mixed.

If you go further south to the Kalahari Desert of South West Africa, some of the African peoples look vaguely Chinese (such as Nelson Mandela). In all cases the African is the prototype and everybody else is the derivative. Therefore it is the Chinese who look like them.

So what?

Suppose an African looking like a narrow featured Somali, Kenyan, Ugandan, or from the desert region of West Africa was depicted in ancient Egyptian sculpture with their hair covered: Would you think the individual depicted was an African or a European?

Some people would mistakenly think they were Europeans. This is why it is important to acknowledge the physical variety that is typically Black, or typically Negro, or typically African.

There is more information on this topic in my book *When We Ruled,* Chapters 4 and 9 (UK, Reklaw Education, 2013, pp.143-153, 326-330).

16. Who else were Black people enslaved by?

Black people were enslaved by the Assyrians towards the end of Egyptian history. In 663 BC the Assyrians conquered and enslaved the Egyptians. In 525 BC the Persians, another Middle Eastern power, conquered and enslaved the Egyptians. In 332 BC the Greeks from southern Europe conquered and enslaved the Egyptians. In 30 BC the Romans conquered and enslaved the Egyptians.

There was however a chapter of Black enslavement that happened even before the Egyptian examples.

There used to be Black civilisations of the Middle East and Asia five thousand years ago. The Sumerians of early Iraq were originally a Black people. Eventually, the Assyrians conquered the remnants of them and reduced them to low status. The Elamites of Iran were originally a Black people. The Persians conquered them and reduced them to servile status. The Dravidians of India and Pakistan created a great Black civilisation. The Aryans conquered them and reduced them to servile status.

Following the Greek conquest of Egypt in 332 BC, we have the Roman conquest of North Africa in 146 BC and completed by 30 BC. The whole of North Africa was conquered by the Romans and they called it 'Africa Romana'. The people that lived there became the slaves of the Romans.

The Arabs conquered North Africa beginning in 639 AD up until 708 AD. The Arabs still rule North Africa today and they are still enslaving Black people. In Sudan the enslavement of Black people is going on right now as also in Mauritania. This is why these countries are having civil wars.

The original people of North Africa were Black people just like us but the Arab conquest cleared those people out. That's why you have find pockets of Black people in the southern parts of all the North African countries. The ones that were left were enslaved and some were sent off to Iraq, to places like Basra. In fact Basra was once an African slave city.

17. Were any other people enslaved like Black people?

When Black people talk about mass enslavement they often forget that the Native Americans were mass murdered. Everybody from Alaska in North America to Chile in South America was originally a Native American. This is not the case now. The millions of Native Americans slaughtered by the Europeans were amongst the worst chapters in human history.

Not enough Black people really talk about this, giving the impression that we were the only ones that suffered.

Even when Europeans wanted to colonise the land taken from the Native Americans the first group of people they tried to enslave were their own working class. However, their populations were not big enough to sustain this and this policy made them politically unpopular at home. That is where the idea came from to visit mass enslavement on African people.

As far as: "Were any other people enslaved like Black people?"

The only comparable group would be the Eastern Europeans. They were enslaved by the Romans, Arabs, Khazars and the Turks. This is why Eastern Europeans are to this day called 'Slavs' (i.e. slaves). Just as slavery has negatively affected the behaviour of Black people, I believe I can show how slavery has negatively affected the behaviour of the Eastern Europeans.

18. Who were the first Black people in America?

In 1858 peasants in Mexico discovered a huge stone head which had African features. In 1862 José Melgar found another one and as more and more diggings occurred more and more huge stone heads were found. Scholars believe that the stone heads date from 1160 BC to 580 BC.

This raised the question: Who were these stone heads depicting?

Clearly the heads depict Africans. There are, however, European scholars that lie about this and claim that the heads do not depict Africans but at the same time they will not actually reproduce the portraits because clearly they are Africans! To answer the question: Which group of Africans? No one really knows. However, various scholars have put forward what I call intelligent theories.

One intelligent theory was put forward by Professor Ivan Van Sertima, the Indian scholar Rafique Ali Jairazbhoy, and a few other writers. They identified the Olmec heads as depicting ancient Egyptians or Sudanese. Professor Van Sertima initially thought the Africans were from the Egyptian 25th Dynasty. Jairazbhoy thought they were from the time of the Egyptian 20th Dynasty. Professor Van Sertima has since changed his mind to be in line with Jairazbhoy. If this is the correct interpretation then the Olmec heads depict Egyptians or Nubians from the time of 20th Dynasty ruler Rameses III. Rafique Ali Jairazbhoy has since written a book called *Rameses III: Father of Ancient America.* This hasn't completely settled the issue because the Olmec heads could be depicting Black people from anywhere.

However while Dr Clyde Ahmad Winters agrees the Olmec heads depict Black people from Africa, he identifies them as a West African ethnic group

Figure 43. This book is available from www.amazon.com

called the Mende instead. Dr Winters' idea is a development of the research of a European American professor called Leo Wiener, who wrote a three volume book in the 1920s called *Africa and the Discovery of America.*

Mr Fari Supiya believes there is just enough evidence to say these Black people could have come to Mexico from Asia and not from Africa. Supiya points out that the people of the Melanesian and Micronesian islands were great sea farers. It is therefore possible that the Olmec heads could well have been depicting them.

To sum up then: There is NO doubt that the people depicted by the Olmec heads were Black people. There is, however, confusion about which country these Black people came from.

There is more information on this topic in my book *Blacks and Science Volume One,* (UK, Reklaw Education, 2013, pp.26-34).

19. How did slavery start?

First of all, let me clarify something. A lot of people talk about transatlantic slavery as if it was a 400 year experience. But if we were being more realistic, Black people have been losing ground for many thousands of years before the transatlantic experience. Black people used to rule Asia Minor and we have since lost that. Similarly we used to rule North Africa but we have also lost that. When we lost control of these territories the remnants of the Black populations were reduced to low status including slavery.

To answer the question, the first slave trader was a Portuguese gentleman called Antam Gonçalves. In 1441 he led the first slave raid against Morocco and kidnapped Africans from the coast at sword point. This event is where scholars traditionally begin retelling the story of mass enslavement. Gonçalves and other Portuguese bandits brought the captives home (to Portugal) and sent others to plantations on Madeira, the Canary Islands and so on.

Word got to Pope Martin V about the Portuguese activities, and he blessed the slave trade, or as he put it, he offered to grant to all those who were engaged in the said war complete forgiveness of their sins! This unfortunately meant that the mass enslavement of Africans was blessed and justified by the Christian Church.

Mass enslavement continued as hit and run raids. There was no buying or selling. However, by the time of 1482, the Portuguese raised their game by over powering the local ruler of the Ghana coast, Kwame Ansa. They forced the building of Elmina Castle and they then colonised the region around it. They enslaved the local Africans to work in and around the Castle.

After 1492 Europeans began taking enslaved people to the Americas. Mass enslavement expanded and the Europeans used their footholds in the African countries where they had a presence to play off the different African groups against each other. This meant that Africans were buying and selling prisoners captured in raids to Europeans in exchange for guns. When that happened, slavery evolved into inter-African warfare that stirred up Black people against Black people.

Holland then got involved in the slave trade and repeated many of the Portuguese actions. They even collected taxes from the local people proving that they had become the government. Again they played off Africans against Africans encouraging warfare, and through that warfare they would get Africans to destroy each other and then collect slaves from both sides.

There is more information on this topic in my book *When We Ruled*, Chapter 18 (UK, Reklaw Education, 2013, pp.624-633).

20. Did Africans profit from slavery?

The simple answer is no.

Mass enslavement worked for Africans like this: You'll find that at any time one African group will be benefiting from slavery but another ten African groups were being raided and slaughtered. It was like a cycle. For the group that is benefiting, their time at the top would be short until it is their time to be raided and slaughtered, and the process would continue.

For the majority of Africans, mass enslavement was an absolute catastrophe. It was so bad that Africa still has not acknowledged it and certainly has not recovered from it. Mass enslavement created huge migrations or refugee problems as large numbers of people were fleeing from being raided. The basis of African tribalism comes from all of these groups being divided and then mixed together, so you would have many different languages being spoken in one area and no individual has any loyalty to the others except members of their own ethnic groups.

Moreover, there were other migrants that could only find sanctuary away from the slave raiders in the caves, the hills and so on. Consequently the culture of these migrants degenerated to the level of cave culture or hill culture. When Europeans colonised Africa over a hundred years ago, they found a lot of people living as naked savages and they were able to use that to justify why they colonised Africa. They claimed to be bringing civilisation. However naked savages haven't always been naked savages. They only became naked savages once mass enslavement began and their culture degenerated because of it.

There is more information on this topic in my book *When We Ruled*, Chapter 18 (UK, Reklaw Education, 2013, pp.622-623, 633-638).

21. Did the Greeks teach the ancient Egyptians or was it the other way round?

The Greeks did not teach the ancient Egyptians. The ancient Egyptian civilisation was already very old and in serious decline when the Greeks came. The beginning of the Greek period was roughly contemporaneous with the Egyptian or Sudanese 25th Dynasty. When the Greeks entered Egypt, there were still knowledgeable Egyptians around. Consequently a lot of Greeks came to Egypt as students.

The ancient Egyptians had an account of creation that the scholars call the 'Heliopolitan Theology'. The creation story begins with the primeval waters of *Nun*. Then we get the first divine principle *Ptah* emerging out the waters in a form of a hill, which is where the Egyptians got their pyramid shape from. On that hill was *Atum Ra*. He is sometimes shown as the sun or as a man. He then created two elements, *Shu* (i.e. air) and *Tefnut* (i.e. water). Shu and Tefnut then reproduce to make *Geb* (i.e. earth) and *Nut* (i.e. sky, fire or perhaps both).

The early Greek philosophers taught that the basic elements of creation were earth, air, fire and water. There is evidence that this is what the Greeks learned while studying in Egypt.

There is more information on this topic in my book *Blacks and Religion Volume One,* (UK, Reklaw Education, 2014, pp.20-32).

22. Who was Ivan Van Sertima and what was his significance?

Ivan Van Sertima was a scholar from Guyana, South America. He was the most productive Black scholar of the 1980s and early 1990s. Initially, he studied Chancellor Williams' book, *The Destruction of Black Civilization.* Following this, he did independent research on the presence of Black people in ancient America during the Olmec period (i.e. the time of Rameses III) and the Mixtec period (i.e. the time of Mansa Abubakari II).

He went on to build a team of scholars and they established *The Journal of African Civilizations.* They put out perhaps a dozen anthologies on

Figure 44. This book is available from www.amazon.com

different aspects of Black history including *Egypt: Child of Africa* and *Great African Thinkers: Volume One* which is dedicated to Cheikh Anta Diop. They put out *African Presence in Early Asia* where they deal with Black civilisations such as the early civilisation of Arabia. They dealt with the Moors in Spain in a volume called *Golden Age of the Moor*. They dealt with Black people in early Crete and early Britain in *African Presence in Early Europe*. They put out *African Presence in Early America* where they expanded on the research topic that Van Sertima began with. They presented an array of evidence which documented the presence of Black people in America in ancient times and medieval times, way before Christopher Columbus got there.

23. Who was Cheikh Anta Diop and what was his significance?

Cheikh Anta Diop is widely regarded as the most important Black historian of the 20th century.

He was born in Senegal in 1923. He went to Paris to study nuclear physics but while he was there, he realized there was more important fish to fry. He therefore became a historian and an Egyptologist.

He submitted a doctorate thesis to the effect that the ancient Egyptians were Black people (unlike the modern Arab Egyptians) but that doctorate thesis was rejected. In 1954 he published his findings anyway. He then did subsequent research and then submitted the doctorate thesis again. After battling the academic establishment in Paris, his thesis was eventually accepted.

In 1974 Diop was one of a number of scholars that took part in something called 'The Cairo Symposium.' Unesco (i.e. United Nations Educational Science and Cultural Organisation) were in the business of trying to put together an eight volume book of the history of Africa. The sticking point was Volume Two dedicated to ancient Egypt. The key issue was: How was Egypt going to be dealt with? Should it be treated as an African civilisation or a non African one?

Unesco called twenty Egyptologists (eighteen Arab & European scholars and two African scholars) to debate the issue. What usually happens when eighteen debate two is that it becomes a massacre but on the contrary, the two massacred the eighteen! Even Unesco had to admit that Diop and his partner had won the argument. To be honest, it made quite funny reading, because the summary of the transcript is published in *Volume Two* of *UNESCO General History of Africa*. So what Diop and his colleague did was to prove the blackness of the Ancient Egyptians. The Symposium is

Figure 45. *L'Afrique Noire Pré-coloniale* (France, 1960).

now regarded as THE moment when contemporary Black scholarship really began.

Professor Diop wrote a book called *Precolonial Black Africa*. This is an English translation of his 1960 classic *L'Afrique Noire Pré-coloniale*.

This book concerns the three great West African empires of Ancient Ghana, Medieval Mali and the Empire of Songhai.

I regard this book as Diop's best book in the English language. It is a wonderful study, and shows the richness of our culture from a cultural perspective, technical perspective, economic perspective, political perspective and a scientific perspective.

24. Were any of the English royal family Black?

Two British royals have major questions marks hanging over them.

There is the 14th century monarch Queen Philippa of Hainault. In all the surviving art of Queen Philippa she looks 100 percent white. However, there is a surviving description by a contemporary foreigner. In the description she is said to be brown skinned with curly hair and all the rest of it. Therefore some scholars believe this individual needs more investigation.

There is also the 18th century Queen of George III, Charlotte Sophia of Mecklenburg. She is thought to be descended from southern European families known to have had Black ancestry. She needs more investigation.

Finally, I read an article in *The Times,* where they revealed the present queen's Black ancestors. The author of the article traced lineages from Queen Elizabeth II back to a Moorish dynasty of the Middle Ages. Again, I would suggest that this needs more research.

25. What was Timbuktu?

Timbuktu was a city in the modern West African nation of Mali. It had a long history dating back to medieval times. The city was founded in the 1100s. By the time we get to the 1300s it was a city with a university population of 25,000 students - which is a lot.

700,000 manuscripts dating back to the university period, or perhaps earlier, still survive today. Modern Black families and institutions in Timbuktu hold these manuscripts in 60 private libraries.

The sorts of things the Timbuktu scholars studied included astrology, astronomy, medicine and surgery. The biggest subject was Islamic law. We know about the different topics and subjects studied because of the content in the manuscript collections that have survived today.

There is more information on this topic in my book *Blacks and Science Volume Two* (UK, Reklaw Education, 2015, pp.21-22, 47-63).

26. What are the many consequences derived from the transatlantic slave industry?

The main consequences concern trans-generational wealth for some, and trans-generational poverty for others.

Transatlantic slavery resulted in a transfer of land, treasures, and other assets from Africans to Europeans. The Europeans have been able to pass

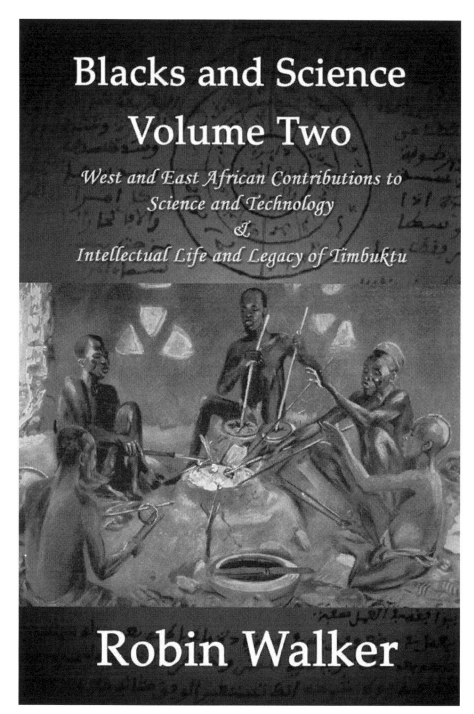

Figure 46. This book is available from www.amazon.com

these forms of wealth down through the generations to the present generation. They have also been able to create institutions and to sustain these institutions across generations to the present generation.

Transatlantic slavery resulted in Black people being stripped of our land, treasures and assets. We have only been able to pass on poverty through the generations to the present generation. We were forcibly prevented from being able to create institutions and we were never able to pass any of this down to the present generation.

With no land, treasures, assets or institutions, we have not been in a position to create employment opportunities. Therefore nearly all of our employment opportunities comes from the white community. They are therefore at liberty to choose whether or not they want to employ you. If they exercise that liberty in a particular way, they can discriminate against you. These actions reinforce poverty in the Black community.

27. Explain the evolution of culture from Blacks being hunters in the jungle to building the great civilizations?

The evolution of culture from savagery to civilisation went like this. 90,000 years ago we know that Africans in (what is now) Congo were the first to engage in fishing. Their fish hooks and other artefacts have been found by archaeologists.

43,000 years ago Africans in what is now Swaziland were the first to have mines and they were digging for a metallic ore. Again, the mines and the stone tools have been found.

25,000 years ago Africans in central Africa were the first to do arithmetic. An artefact called the Ishango Bone was found with evidence of a numerical system carved into it.

15,000 years ago Africans in the Kenyan hills were the first to domesticate animals because animal bones have been found in a restricted zone which showed that humans controlled those animals.

12,000 years ago Africans in the Nubian Sahara were the first to plant crops.

By the time we get to 7900 years ago we get the world's first civilisation which was the ancient Nubian Kingdom of Ta-Seti. This was the first organised government in the world.

When we get to 7600 years ago, we get the world's second civilisation - ancient Egypt.

There is more information on this topic in my book *When We Ruled,* Chapter 5 and the Afterword (UK, Reklaw Education, 2013, pp.166-173, 750-752).

28. What were some of the great civilisations in North Africa?

One of the great civilisations in North Africa was Carthage. It existed in modern day Tunisia. The time period for Carthage was 814 BC to 146 BC. The capital city, also known as Carthage, had 700,000 people living there at its highest. It had six storey villas, public baths and theatres.

The Carthaginian Empire was not just in Tunisia. It also controlled the islands of Majorca, Sardinia, and a whole chunk of Africa and so on. It was a very large and powerful empire. Its greatest ruler was Hannibal, the brilliant and daring soldier, who used elephants as tanks.

The Carthaginian Empire was eventually conquered by the Romans in 146 BC.

There is more information on this topic in my book *When We Ruled,* Chapter 10 (UK, Reklaw Education, 2013, pp.348-369).

29. Were there great civilisations in Southern Africa?

The two most important civilisations in southern Africa was the Kingdom of Great Zimbabwe which then evolved into the Empire of Munhumutapa (also called 'Monomotapa').

Great Zimbabwe is now a ruined city from which the modern country of Zimbabwe took its name. The standing ruins consist of 12 stone buildings, within which there was evidence of cottages. On the basis of the cottages, scholars estimate that the city had between 18,000 and 25,000 people living there. If we compare this to London of the 14th century, London had 20,000 people living there so we're talking about the same sort of size.

Archaeologists have found the gold mines that the people of Great Zimbabwe worked. In ancient and medieval times they cleaned out those gold mines. Scholars estimate that the early miners shifted a staggering 43 1/4 million tons of ore!!!

What is interesting is that the outcrop was so hard that you would need dynamite to blast through the reef, yet these African miners were digging to a depth of 150 feet and clearing the huge quantity of ore!

There is more information on this topic in my book *When We Ruled,* Chapter 17 (UK, Reklaw Education, 2013, pp.592-618).

Figure 47. Some of the ruined buildings that comprise the Great Zimbabwe Temple.

30. Who was responsible for ending the Slave Trade?

The Slave Trade came to an end because of a number of uprisings or rebellions. The most important of which took place in Haiti.

In 1791 a Jamaican called Bookman Dutty began to get the people of Haiti into a frame of mind to start the rebellion. He was a priest of an African deity called Ogun which was associated with war and iron. On 14th August 1791 he got the people involved in an Ogun ceremony which fired them up and got them ready to fight.

Eight days later, the revolution against the French enslavers began. Bookman Dutty was eventually captured and killed. Thus leadership of the revolution of the enslaved people passed to Toussaint L'Ouverture. Eventually leadership then passed to Jean Jacques Dessalines. He completed the revolution and proclaimed Haiti to be a free black republic in 1803.

The various French people responsible for mass enslavement were rounded up and executed.

In 1806 and 1807 various countries in Europe began to loosen their grip on the Slave Trade. Britain banned the movement of enslaved people on British ships because they were worried that if a repeat of Haiti happened, other Europeans might end up being executed. Eventually, other countries started to abolish the movement of enslaved people but slavery itself continued.

In 1831 the Jamaican revolutionary leader Sam Sharpe led a rebellion which Caribbean historians now call the 'Emancipation War'. That resulted in Britain passing an abolition act in 1834. They didn't implement it until 1838 which is where we get the abolition of slavery in the English speaking colonies.

In 1848 the same thing happened in the French speaking colonies.

In 1865 the same thing happened in the United States and the story continued until 1888 when we get the final abolition in the last of the Spanish speaking colonies.

There is more information on this topic in my book *When We Ruled*, Chapter 18 (UK, Reklaw Education, 2013, pp.639-651).

31. What do we know about Black people in 18th century England?

There were great Black personalities such as Phyllis Wheatley, a poetess. She wrote a collection known as *Poems on Various Subjects*. Her poetry is quite good but it does have a 'redeemed and saved' quality where she is almost glad she became a slave because slavery brought her away from the 'pagans' of Africa! This is a little embarrassing to read but some of her poetry is still interesting.

Figure 48. Phyllis Wheatley.

The Black Musical Tradition
AND
Early Black Literature

Robin Walker

Figure 49. This book is available from www.amazon.com

Another important 18th century personality was Ignatius Sancho, who, together with his wife, opened a grocery shop in Westminster. He was also an author of letters that became best sellers and also musical compositions. Now let us be clear what we mean. We mean 18th century classical music!

Another famous Black person in the 18th century was Oludah Equiano. He was considered the leader of the African community and he would hold his political meetings at the Church of St Martin in the Fields (which is quite close to Charing Cross tube station). His political movement was called the Sons of Africa. They wrote letters to Parliament trying to agitate for the abolition of slavery.

There is more information on Phyllis Wheatley in my book *The Black Musical Tradition and Early Black Literature* (UK, Reklaw Education, 2015, pp.74-77).

32. What do we know about Black people in 19th century England?

One famous personality in 19th century England was William Cuffay. Cuffay was a member of the left wing radicals at the time, known as the Chartists. It must be remembered that Karl Marx had not written his *Manifesto of the Communist Party* at this point, so this was before the communist movement was born. The Chartists were left wing radicals who agitated for the rights of working people. One of its leaders was Cuffay. His name Cuffay indicates that his ancestry is probably from the Ghana region (Cf. Cuffay and 'Kofi'). Cuffay was arrested along with many of the Chartist leaders because they were considered subversives. Eventually, he was deported to Tasmania. However, it is interesting that even in Tasmania he continued to be a radical. He continued to agitate for working class rights.

Another Black icon in the 19th century was the actor Ira Aldridge. Ira Aldridge was born in America and came to study in a Scottish university. He developed an interest in Shakespearian plays and became a Shakespearian actor, becoming active on the London stage. However, unfavourable critical reaction lead to him leaving London to tour Europe. In Europe he was worshipped! The German critics claimed he was the greatest tragic actor the Berlin public had ever seen. In Switzerland and Poland he received accolades. He also married a Polish countess. In Russia he was a guest of the Tsar, the ruler of Russia. In Asiatic Russia he was made an Associate of the Order of Nobles, which was the highest accolade an artist could possibly receive. If we were to look at a list of his

Figure 50. Ira Aldridge.

achievements it is difficult to see a 20th century actor that has achieved anything like it. Possibly the closest might be Sidney Poitier.

33. What do we know about Black people in 20th century England?

There is a chapter in Black British history that most Black British people have never heard of. That chapter concerns the rise of Pan Africanism (1900 to 1945).

By the time we get to the 20th century, most of Africa had been colonised by Europe. Most Black people were either ex slaves or the colonised subjects of Europeans. Thus London became the centre of Pan-African ideas where Black people would come together to fight against this.

In the year 1900 a Black man from Trinidad called Henry Sylvester Williams organised the first Pan African Conference to challenge the idea of European colonisation of Africans. It was him that coined the phrase 'Pan-African'. At the conference he held in London, Black Londoners were there. The most famous composer in England at the time was there. He was a Black man and professor of music at Trinity College called Samuel Coleridge Taylor. Another important attendee was a young Dr Du Bois coming over from America. It was at that conference that Du Bois delivered his famous speech that the problem of the 20th century was going to be the colour line, i.e. the relationship between the lighter races to the darker races. What is interesting is that Dr Du Bois was absolutely correct in that prediction.

Eventually Dr Du Bois would take over the Pan-African movement and would lead it, but again, many of the early conferences took place in Britain. One of the most famous was held in Manchester in 1945. Many of the people who went on to lead post independence Africa were in attendance at this conference such as Dr Kwame Nkrumah.

I have since met some of the elders who remember that conference and who were there. They were surprised that relatively 'young' people like me would be interested in things like that.

There is more information on this topic in my book *When We Ruled,* Chapter 18 (UK, Reklaw Education, 2013, pp.653-654).

Figure 51. *Africa & Orient Review,* April 1920.

34. Is it true that a Black newspaper operated in Fleet Street, London?

There was a black newspaper called the *Africa & Orient Review*. It operated from 158 Fleet Street in Central London. Its staff members were about half African and half Caribbean and one or two Hindus. The founder of the paper was a Black man from Egypt called Duse Mohammed Ali. I personally have a reproduction of a 1920 edition of the paper.

What is interesting about the paper is that it had the symbols of the pharaoh on the front cover. This made it clear what the ideology of the paper was.

The articles were very long and thoughtful. Today they would be considered 'Afrocentric.' They published articles on the roles of Black people in history, reviews of actors such as Ira Aldridge, and all different types of topics came up.

35. What differences are there with immersing ourselves in ancient Black mathematics and science compared to already established western sciences?

I work on the principle that the more you know is the more you can do. Many of us learned arithmetic especially multiplication by learning our times tables. What is interesting, however, is that the ancient Egyptians and Ethiopians had ways of multiplying and dividing large numbers that did not require you to learn the times tables. Now if you knew that Egyptian system you could add that to your armoury so you have many more ways of doing things.

That is not just true of mathematics but true of all the sciences and the arts, and all the forms of architecture and engineering. The more you know, the more you can do.

Another important point is that what we today consider to be modern sciences are not always modern. A lot of people who have been credited for creating new scientific ideas did not deserve that credit.

For example Charles Darwin is said to be the founder of the natural selection theory of evolution. Natural selection is the idea that different members of the same species have slightly different characteristics. If a particular characteristic adds to the evolutionary advantage of that species that particular trait ends up becoming more and more dominant over generations. Consequently the population as a whole will change towards that particular trait that gets selected for. There is competition for resources

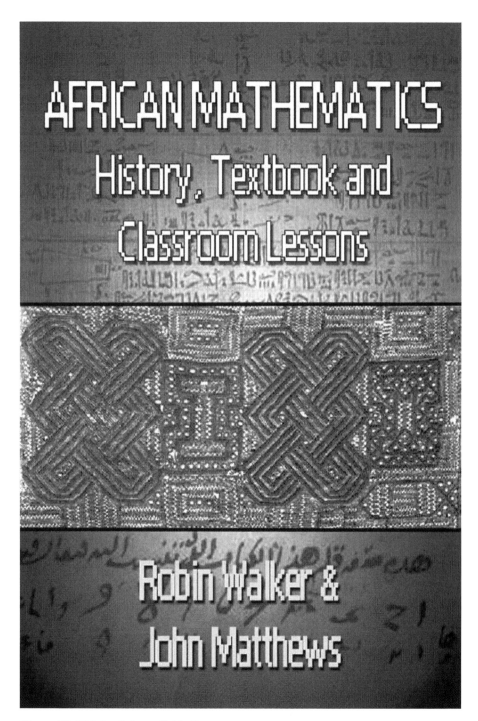

Figure 52. This book is available from www.amazon.com

and those that are the fittest will end up out-competing the others. Therefore the population will change over generations in favour of that particular advantaged group.

Darwin, however, was not the first person to say this. There was a Black Arab scholar from the 9th century called Al Jahiz (also written as 'Al Jahith') who also wrote a book with the modest title *The Book of the Glory of the Blacks over the Whites.* Not only was Al Jahiz the first scholar to explain the theory of natural selection (in *The Book of Animals*); it is interesting to note that scholars are now beginning to admit and discuss this fact.

I discuss Ancient Egyptian and Ethiopian mathematics in my book (co authored with John Matthews) *African Mathematics: History, Textbook and Classroom Lessons* (UK, Reklaw Education, 2014, pp.13-39, 48-61). I discuss Al Jahiz in my book *The Black Musical Tradition and Early Black Literature* (UK, Reklaw Education, 2015, pp.57-58).

36. Who was W. E. B. Du Bois and why is he important to Black people?

Dr W. E. B. Du Bois is important for a number of reasons (See also question 33) but I am only interested in W. E. B. Du Bois the historian. In 1915 he wrote a book called *The Negro* and that book sketched out the early history of the African. There is a lot you can fault in the book but the point is he laid out the model. In the 1930s he fattened up the book which now became *Black Folk Now and Then.* In 1946 he fattened up the book again into *The World and Africa.* This book is a classic and his perspective is broad.

He has a discussion of the African origins of the human race. Also there is a discussion of the civilisation he calls 'Ethiopia' and Egypt which on a modern map would be Sudan and Egypt. He has a discussion of Hannibal of Carthage, a discussion of the West African empires of Ghana, Mali and Songhai. He also has an account of the Central African empires, Medieval Nubia, and the southern African empires of Zimbabwe and Munhumutapa. He also attempts to integrate some of the East African civilisations such as the Swahili Confederation. He does not do this particularly well but let us be clear, he is a pioneer. We also get an account of the Black civilizations of early Asia such as the Sumerian civilisation of early Iraq and the Dravidian civilization of pre historic India and Pakistan. The book itself then goes into a discussion of mass enslavement and tries to bring the story up to date.It remains a major landmark.

Figure 53. Here we have it! *Volume 2.*

37. Who was Drusilla Houston and why is she important to Black history?

Drusilla Dunjee Houston was a pioneering scholar. She was one of the big three historians from the 1920s generation (the other two were J. A. Rogers and William Leo Hansberry). She was the first Black Orientalist. The Orientalists study the ancient civilisations of 'the East' particularly Egypt, the Middle East, Arabia, all the way across to India. The book she wrote was called *Wonderful Ethiopians of the Ancient Cushite Empire: Volume 1* which came out in 1926.

Very recently African American scholar Dr Peggy Brooks-Bertram found a manuscript of volume two and has since edited and reprinted it. *Volume 2* covers the same ground as *Volume 1* but with more documentation.

Drusilla Houston's work, in my opinion, is brilliant and very advanced. However, not all scholars agree and I have heard a lot of disparaging things from some of our most respected scholars on Drusilla Houston. As I said, her stuff is brilliant and she deserves respect for being the first Black scholar to delve into the Orientalist territory and gain mastery over that material. Moreover, some of her accounts, such as her account on the ancient Black civilisation in the Arabian peninsular have hardly been bettered by later scholars.

38. Who was J. A. Rogers and why is he important to Black history?

J. A. Rogers was a historian of Jamaican origins. He was one of the big three historians from the 1920s generation (the other two were Drusilla Houston and William Leo Hansberry). His main interest was to document the history of racial admixture involving the Black race.

His three volume work on *Sex and Race* traced the history of racial admixture in Early Africa, the Middle East, Europe, Asia, North America and South America.

His book, *Nature Knows No Color Line,* contained some of the best research and documentation of the Moors in Spain by any scholar.

Finally, his two-volume work, *World's Great Men of Color,* contained biographies and short accounts of great Black and mixed-race people on all continents, throughout history.

The great historian, Dr Runoko Rashidi, is very much influenced by J. A. Rogers' work. Portions of Dr Ben's books are also commentaries on J. A. Rogers' work.

39. Who was J. C. DeGraft-Johnson and why was he important to Black history?

John Coleman DeGraft-Johnson was a historian from Ghana. He is best known for his book *African Glory* which was published in 1954. The book is a classic and contains accounts of the rise and fall of ancient Egypt, the Empire of Carthage, the North African church, the West African Empires of Ghana, Mali and Songhai, and the Moors in Spain.

He also has a good account of the Kingdom of Kongo and a fair account of the Empire of Munhumutapa. Professor DeGraft-Johnson also has an account of the Slave Trade.

The book remains massively influential. *The Great and Mighty Walk* documentary featuring Professor John Henrik Clarke was heavily influenced by DeGraft-Johnson's perspective. Portions of Dr Ben's books are virtually commentaries on DeGraft-Johnson's book. Finally Professor John Jackson's *Introduction to African Civilizations* is also influenced by DeGraft-Johnson's work.

40. Who is Dr Ben and why is he important to Black history?

Dr Ben also known as Yosef ben Jochannan is a really interesting elder scholar. He is of Ethiopian descent and his family is connected to the Falasha Jews of Ethiopia.

His focus is on challenging not just racist bias in history but also religious bias in history. His theory is because ancient civilisations such as Egypt, Kush, and Ethiopia, are also connected to Judaism, Christianity, and Islam; it is not just white supremacy that has tried to write us out of history. In his view, religious bigots have ALSO tried to write us out of history for the same reasons.

His most important books are *Black Man of the Nile and His Family* and *Africa Mother of Western Civilization*. These books are primarily focused on Egyptology and Nile Valley studies with chapters on Great Zimbabwe, Carthage and commentaries on the books of J. A. Rogers, Basil Davidson, and John Coleman DeGraft-Johnson.

Dr Ben's strength is he challenges the prevailing racist ideas that try to disconnect Negroes from ancient Egypt. One common racist theory is the 'True Negro' hypothesis which claims that the ONLY Black people in Africa are West Africans! Dr Bens' books slaughter this ludicrous idea. (See also question 15 which is based on Dr Ben's research).

Dr Ben has also written a series of books called T*he Black Man's Religion: Volumes 1, 2* and *3*. In these volumes he shows that Judaism, Christianity and Islam and many of the beliefs within those religions, such as their creation stories, are derived directly from African sources. He is clear that there were Asian sources too but he is highlighting the African sources. For example when he deals with Judaism, his chapter is called 'Moses: African Influences in Judaism'. Now the prophet Moses, if he existed at all, entered history in a basket floating down the Egyptian Nile. He was therefore an Egyptian. With Christianity, one of its fathers was St Augustine who was African. With Islam one of its fathers was Bilal who was also an African.

When it comes to modern religions and modern religious leaders, Dr Ben documents the role of Sweet Daddy Grace who was an African American religious leader. There was also the Moorish Science Temple of America, the Nation of Islam, and powerful individuals like Dr Martin Luther King. This again shows that Black people were not just movers and shakers in religion back in the day but we are movers and shakers today.

41. Who is Ashra Kwesi and why is he important to Black history?

Ashra Kwesi is an Egyptologist. He was a student of Dr Ben and has developed Dr Ben's research into Egyptology and also the African origin of religion.

Kwesi leads study tours to Egypt. His focus is on linking the ancient Egyptian religion to the later religions of Judaism and Christianity. Most Black scholars follow the precedent set by Professor John Jackson and Dr Charles Finch. Their research is largely based on the scholarship of the early 20th century English scholars, Gerald Massey and his student Albert Churchward.

Ashra Kwesi's approach is very different. He shows the links DIRECTLY from the imagery on the ancient Egyptian temple walls to Judaic and Christian beliefs. This completely bypasses the research of Massey and Churchward. This approach has made Kwesi the leading Black scholar in the world in these topic areas.

It is unfortunate that he has not yet written a book on his research.

42. Who do you think is the most important scholar to explain the fall of Africa?

Dr Chancellor Williams was the most important scholar to explain the fall of Africa. He was a professor at Howard University and his education was in the social sciences generally including economics, sociology and history. His most important book is *The Destruction of Black Civilization* which was originally published in 1971 and reworked in 1974. What is on sale right now is the 1987 edition. The book is a masterpiece but not all of the scholarship is even. This was because Dr Williams was going blind while the book was being written so some sections were rushed. However, when the book is on point, it's on point. It contains some of the very best ever research and analysis into our history.

What Williams showed is how mass enslavement and its history played off African peoples against other African peoples. Once you end up doing that, you don't just have a situation where we are fighting each other, you also end up with the resulting enmity still being there hundreds of years later. This resulted in the key reason why Africa is as divided as it is. Dr Chancellor Williams explains this very well indeed.

All that I would add is that some of his details need correcting but the basic model is very much correct! (See also question 20 which is very much based on Williams' research).

43. What year was Malcolm X assassinated?

Malcolm X was killed in the year 1965. This was one year after leaving the Nation of Islam to form the Organization of Afro-American Unity. This was the American branch of the Organisation of African Unity.

No one knows for sure who was behind the assassination of Malcolm X but members of the Nation of Islam were jailed for it.

44. When did Abraham Lincoln issue his Emancipation Proclamation?

Abraham Lincoln gave his famous speech in 1863 which declared freedom to enslaved African Americans.

This, however, remains controversial indeed.

The United States was embroiled in a civil war. The Emancipation Proclamation only applied to the enslaved Africans who were on the opposing side to the side controlled by Abraham Lincoln! The Emancipation Proclamation was designed to inconvenience the opposing side. Since Lincoln had no power to enforce this over his opponents, the Emancipation Proclamation had no impact whatsoever and freed no slaves.

The mass enslavement of African Americans actually ended in 1865 after the civil war came to an end. Slavery was prohibited in the United States by the 13th Amendment to the American Constitution.

45. What is this thing I'm always hearing about: Kwanzaa?

Kwanza means 'first fruits' in the East African language of Swahili. It was originally a harvest festival.

Kwanzaa (notice the extra 'a') is a seven day festival derived from the East African harvest that is celebrated by some African Americans and other Black peoples across the globe. It starts on the 26th of December and ends on the 1st of January.

Kwanzaa was started in 1966 by an African American scholar and activist, Professor Maulana Karenga. From small beginnings, Kwanzaa is increasing in popularity each year having spread across the globe. The festival promotes Black or African unity and culture. It is also based on seven principles known as the Nguzo Saba. Each of the seven principles is highlighted on each of the seven days: one day per principle.

46. Where was the first organised protest against slavery in America?

The first organised protest against slavery in America was in Germantown in February 1688. Germantown is now a part of Philadelphia in Pennsylvania. The leaders of the protest were four white Quakers. Francis Pastorius drew up the petition document and three other Quakers signed it.

47. What American state was the first to abolish slavery?

Vermont was the first American state to abolish slavery in 1777. Slavery was specifically abolished in the constitution that Vermont adopted on 8 July 1777.

48. When did Black History Month actually start?

Black History Month began life as Negro History Week. Professor Carter Woodson, a pioneering African American historian, started it in 1926. In time Negro History Week evolved into Black History Month which is celebrated in both the United States and Canada in the month of February.

Akyaaba Addai Sebbo is one of two names that are mentioned in the birth of Black History Month in the UK. Another person who may have been responsible was the Labour politician, Linda Bellos.

Black History Month in the UK has been a regular fixture since 1987 and is celebrated in October rather than in February.

49. Who is Clifford Alexander?

Clifford Alexander was the first US Army Secretary. He was appointed by President Jimmy Carter in 1977 and he was also saluted at the Pentagon. He served for about 4 years. During this time, he increased the number of Black army generals from about 12 to 30, including the first Black woman.

In 1981 he founded Alexander & Associates. This is a consulting firm that advises corporations on workforce inclusiveness.

Clifford Alexander also serves on the boards of Mutual of America Life Insurance Company and several Dreyfus mutual funds. He has been chairman and CEO of the Dun & Bradstreet Corporation, and chairman of Moody's Corporation.

50. When did the American parliament pass the Fugitive Slave Law?

They passed the law in 1850 with only four members opposing it! Abolitionists, however, nicknamed it the 'Bloodhound Law' since dogs were used to track down runaway slaves.

The law stated that any federal marshal who did not arrest an alleged runaway slave could be fined $1,000. Similarly, anyone who aided a runaway slave was liable to be imprisoned.

Individuals suspected of being a runaway slave could be arrested and turned over to a claimant on nothing more than his sworn testimony of ownership. A suspected runaway could not ask for a trial against being a suspected slave nor could they testify in court on his or her own behalf.

PART THREE

THE AUTHOR

ROBIN WALKER

1. Biography

Robin Walker 'The Black History Man' was born in London but has also lived in Jamaica. He attended the London School of Economics and Political Science where he read Economics.

In 1991 and 1992, he studied African World Studies with the brilliant Dr Femi Biko and later with Mr Kenny Bakie. Between 1993 and 1994, he trained as a secondary school teacher at Edge Hill College (linked to the University of Lancaster).

Since 1992 and up to the present period, Robin Walker has lectured in adult education, taught university short courses, and chaired conferences in African World Studies, Egyptology and Black History. The venues have been in Toxteth (Liverpool), Manchester, Leeds, Bradford, Huddersfield, Birmingham, Cambridge, Buckinghamshire and London.

Since 1994 he has taught Economics, Business & Finance, Mathematics, Information Communications Technology, PSHE/Citizenship and also History at various schools in London and Essex.

In 1999 he wrote *Classical Splendour: Roots of Black History* published in the UK by Bogle L'Ouverture Publications. In the same year, he co-authored (with Siaf Millar) *The West African Empire of Songhai,* a textbook used by many schools across the country.

In 2000 he co-authored (again with Siaf Millar) *Sword, Seal and Koran,* another book on the Songhai Empire of West Africa.

In 2006 he wrote the seminal *When We Ruled.* This was the most advanced synthesis on Ancient and Mediaeval African history ever written by a single author. It was a massive expansion of his earlier book *Classical Splendour: Roots of Black History* and established his reputation as the leading Black History educational service provider.

In 2008 he wrote *Before The Slave Trade,* a highly pictorial companion volume to *When We Ruled.*

Between 2011 and 2014 he wrote a series of e-books for download sold through Amazon Kindle. These e-books covered history, business, religion, music, and science.

In 2013, he co-authored (with Siaf Millar and Saran Keita) *Everyday Life In An Early West African Empire*. It was a massive expansion on the earlier book *Sword, Seal & Koran*. He updated *When We Ruled* by incorporating nearly all of the images from *Before The Slave Trade*. He wrote a trilogy of books entitled *Blacks and Science Volumes One, Two* and *Three*.

In 2014, he wrote *The Rise and Fall of Black Wall Street and the Seven Key Empowerment Principles, Blacks and Religion Volume One* and the book that you are holding right now.

In 2015 he wrote *The Black Musical Tradition and Early Black Literature*.

Speaking Engagements

Looking for a speaker for your next event?

The author Robin Walker 'The Black History Man' is dynamic and engaging, both as a speaker and a workshop leader. He brings Black or African history alive, making it relevant for the present generation. You will love his perfect blend of accessibility, engagement, and academic rigour where learning becomes fun.

Walker is available to give speaking engagements to a variety of audiences. One of his most popular lectures is *When We Ruled: Thousands of Years of a Visible African Heritage*. Another relevant lecture is *The Lost Civilisations of Central Africa*.

To book Robin Walker for your next event, send an email to historicalwalker@yahoo.com

INDEX

Printed in Great Britain
by Amazon